# Leading for Transformational Change

# Leading for Transformational Change

## Case Studies to Show Effective Decision-Making

Wafa Hozien

PUBLISHED IN PARTNERSHIP WITH THE AMERICAN
ASSOCIATION OF SCHOOL ADMINISTRATORS

THE SCHOOL SUPERINTENDENTS ASSOCIATION

ROWMAN & LITTLEFIELD
*Lanham • Boulder • New York • London*

Published in partnership with the American Association of School Administrators
Published by Rowman & Littlefield

An imprint of The Rowman & Littlefield Publishing Group, Inc.
4501 Forbes Boulevard, Suite 200, Lanham, Maryland 20706
www.rowman.com

86–90 Paul Street, London EC2A 4NE

Copyright © 2022 by Wafa Hozien

*All rights reserved.* No part of this book may be reproduced in any form or by any electronic or mechanical means, including information storage and retrieval systems, without written permission from the publisher, except by a reviewer who may quote passages in a review.

British Library Cataloguing in Publication Information Available

**Library of Congress Cataloging-in-Publication Data**

Names: Hozien, Wafa, author.
Title: Leading for transformational change : case studies to show effective decision-making / Wafa Hozien.
Description: Lanham : Rowman & Littlefield, [2022] | Includes bibliographical references.
Identifiers: LCCN 2022032536 (print) | LCCN 2022032537 (ebook) | ISBN 9781475842494 (cloth) | ISBN 9781475842500 (paperback) | ISBN 9781475842517 (epub)
Subjects: LCSH: School management and organization—United States—Decision making—Case studies. | School superintendents—Vocational guidance—United States—Case studies. | Educational leadership—United States—Case studies.
Classification: LCC LB2806 .H69 2022 (print) | LCC LB2806 (ebook) | DDC 371.200973—dc23/eng/20220908
LC record available at https://lccn.loc.gov/2022032536
LC ebook record available at https://lccn.loc.gov/2022032537

This book is dedicated to all of you out there that have worked beyond the school day. You stayed long hours, way above your contractual duties, to ensure the well-being of our students and their families.

To the Hozien Family

For my father, Ismail, who loved me so much and was always proud of me.

For that amazing mother that everyone should have, Zakieh Hozien

For my beloved brothers—Muhammad, Abdulmajeed, Nidal—and their families

For always nudging me forward this book is dedicated to the beacon in my life:

For my children—Hana, Imam Ismail, Isra, and Mahmoud

Thank you all for being a treasure to beholden to, you outshine me in every way!

# Contents

| | | |
|---|---|---|
| Foreword | | ix |
| Acknowledgments | | xi |
| Introduction | | xiii |
| 1 | Our Mission, Vision, and Values Encompass Who We Are | 1 |
| | Case Study: The Trauma-Informed Care Initiative 1 | |
| | Case Study: Zero Means Zero 4 | |
| | Case Study: A Personal Philosophy for the Public 7 | |
| | Case Study: White Flight 9 | |
| | Case Study: Defining Moments 11 | |
| 2 | Coming to Terms with Ethics in Our Profession | 17 |
| | Case Study: Changing the Schools to Prison Pipeline 18 | |
| | Case Study: What's in a Name? 23 | |
| | Case Study: Finances First 26 | |
| | Case Study: Every Child Matters 29 | |
| | Case Study: Tomatoe, Tomato, What's Your Imago? 32 | |
| 3 | Creating a Sense of Belonging, Inclusivity in a Post-Pandemic World | 37 |
| | Case Study: Low Income, High Expectations 38 | |
| | Case Study: Preparing for Diversity 40 | |
| | Case Study: How We've Always Done It 43 | |
| | Case Study: Emotional and Behavioral Disorders (EBD) in Pine Tree 47 | |
| | Case Study: Period Shaming 49 | |

| | | |
|---|---|---|
| **4** | Creating Communities to Champion All Students<br>Case Study: Navigating Chartered Waters 54<br>Case Study: Getting Them All across the Stage 56<br>Case Study: To V or Not to V 58<br>Case Study: Back to School 60<br>Case Study: Separate but Equal 63 | 53 |
| **5** | Cultivating Meaningful Professional Engagement for the Communities We Lead<br>Case Study: But They Have a Long Runway 68<br>Case Study: Sure Shots 71<br>Case Study: Evaluation Devaluation 74<br>Case Study: More than Money 77<br>Case Study: Bonding with the Community 79 | 67 |
| **6** | Supporting Sustainable School Improvement<br>Case Study: Be My Guest 84<br>Case Study: Continuous Improvement Begins Here 87<br>Case Study: Reading between the Lines 89<br>Case Study: What's in a Grade? 92<br>Case Study: Social Media Threat 94 | 83 |

| | |
|---|---|
| Appendix A: Possible Resolutions | 97 |
| References | 119 |
| Bibliography | 123 |
| About the Author | 126 |

# Foreword

A strong leader can have an impact on an organization for many years to come. In education, a strong superintendent can impact the culture that touches the lives of many: those that they come into contact with and those that they do not. As we emerge into a post-pandemic world, I have noticed increased attention and discussion on matters related to diversity, equity, and inclusion or DEI. In regard to leadership, the matter of DEI is most related to competency and proactive steps toward promoting inclusivity. As someone who teaches in an educational leadership preparation program, I am thrilled whenever a book comes along that addresses the need for leaders to be proactive in improving student learning outcomes for all students.

This book is presented through school district level case studies that provide insight into creative ways for improving student performance and school productivity. By writing on and examining the case studies of school districts, Dr. Hozien is able to illustrate to the reader the importance of understanding organizational systems and most importantly, the role of responsive leadership in dealing with the myriad of complex issues a district faces.

The need for having a grasp on these timely and relevant issues related to student success is urgent. Our society is increasingly becoming diverse, and we cannot afford to leave any child behind, regardless of race, ethnicity, social class, and so on, for whatever reason. Having an understanding of the contemporary issues afflicting our school districts related to learning and achievement, as well as being equipped with the knowledge and leadership ability to adequately confront the challenges, is paramount. The real-life examples presented before you in this book offer the reader a tool for learning about these pressing educational issues in hopes they can enact the necessary changes to deliver a quality education for all. That is why this book should be required reading and an integral part of all the school leadership preparation programs.

I congratulate Dr. Wafa Hozien on her book, *School Superintendent Case Studies: Leading for Transformational Change*. This book will without question add to the body of work on superintendents and leadership, but with a flare of inclusivity.

Dr. Jeff Wilson, Associate Professor

Virginia Commonwealth University

Richmond, VA 23284

# Acknowledgments

This book is dedicated to the three women who made me who I am today: Zakieh, Hana, and Isra. To my mother, Zakieh, thank you for giving me space to be me, even if you haven't always understood why. Thank you for always pushing me academically and never allowing me to settle for less. Thank you for stepping in to help raise my two older children, even when I did not ask you to. I carry the ancestral wisdom passed on through the ages, as embodied by my mother Zakieh, in my heart wherever I go.

For Hana, for your emotional and intellectual support when I needed to journey off to England, and all the other times you were around helping at home. You did all this to make sure I knew that I was loved and was extraordinary. I really would not be here without your love and support. You have kept me grounded.

To my biggest cheerleader, my beloved daughter, Isra, thank you. I would not have made it through the writing of this book without you and your edits. You made so many sacrifices, big and small, from coming to every campus and conference with me. You have overcome insurmountable hurdles in helping me get to where I need to be; stories will be told of our past and ongoing journeys.

I am so humbled to have such an amazing blood family, and chosen family, who have supported me in all my endeavors. To Muhammad, my oldest brother, thank you for being a possibility model for me and for constantly reminding me why my work is important. To Valerie, thank you for grabbing me by the arm and forcing me to stand on my own as a scholar. And to my brother, Abdulmajeed, who is my rock and supporter: I love you, "big bro"! You always nudged me forward; for that I remain insurmountably grateful. To Khadijeh, thank you for being the family rock and offering your guidance. Thank you to my brother, Nidal. I am grateful to you for all your support over the past years. Words cannot state how appreciative I am for all that you do for my children and Mama. To Tagreed, you were the first person that I know who always made me feel welcomed and always brings a smile to my face with your jokes.

To Ismail who has shown me kindness and who I know will continue to be a light in this world. Thank you for your wisdom and guidance beyond your years. I am thankful for your fierce advocacy, for helping me stay centered and reminding me that there is life outside of the academy. I am grateful to Mahmoud for his insightful feedback. To Mahmoud, thank you for helping to stretch my thinking in ways I never thought possible. Thank you for all the kisses and for being one of my biggest cheerleaders.

To Fatimah, thank you for making sure everything behind the scenes runs smoothly, ensuring I got the support I needed, for being a sympathetic ear and opening the doors to your home when I needed a place to stay. And to all my other nieces and nephews: Ismail, Maram, Ahmad, Aymen, Serene, Muhammad, Zakieh, and Layann, go forth and bring greatness to this world, as you already have done to mine.

To my brilliant, bold, unapologetic children, I love you, and you continue to inspire me to do this work. Thank you for allowing me to spread my wings while I pursue my own dreams. I wouldn't have been able to do this without your support and encouragement. You are my heart.

*A special thank you* goes to Natalie R. Desiderio, my administrative assistant who worked diligently on the many graphs in this book to meet my deadlines. Thank you is not enough for the help you do for me.

# Introduction

Emerging leaders, especially those within our schools, require continuing education and training to contend with the changing nature of education and the evolving instruction, curriculum, and administrative requirements of teaching children. Therefore, preparing adult learners to become thoughtful leaders is integral to the success of our schools and our children's future. According to Schumacher (2013), case-based learning in an adult learning environment "bridges the gap for leaders between theoretical knowledge and real-life work situations." In addition, case-based learning (CBL) affords students the opportunity to apply their knowledge to real-world scenarios, thus promoting higher levels of cognition per Bloom's Taxonomy (Yale Poorvu Center for Teaching and Learning 2021).

Especially now more than ever before, while residing in a post-pandemic world, educational leaders need to have more exposure to experiences leading them to make informed quick decisions. This book is a first step in cultivating a healthy decision-making process. Utilizing case studies in educational settings encourages future educational leaders to read, analyze, discuss, confer, and arrive at conclusions regarding the best course of action (Schumacher 2013) and allows students to visualize what they would do in a similar situation to prepare or anticipate the appropriate response should a similar circumstance occur for them. As a result, case study methodology is beneficial in preparing school superintendents to be successful in their roles by responding to practical scenarios that they soon could face (Hozien 2019).

## CASE-BASED LEARNING (CBL) FRAMEWORK

Nath (2005) explained that education has a long history of using case study methodology as a teaching tool dating as far back as John Dewey's philosophy of "real-world" application. Case studies were first predominantly used in law schools and legal judgments (Çakmak and Akgün 2018). There are varying definitions of and delineations between case study and case study methodology. Kowalski (2011) explains that the case study is a scenario, while case study methodology is using that scenario as a teaching paradigm.

The World Association for Case Method Research & Application, founded in 1984, advocates for using the case method in teaching, training, and planning because the approach facilitates critical thinking and group work. Schiano and Andersen (2017) assert that case study teaching can be effective in an online learning environment, becoming more crucial in this day and age of COVID-19.

According to Hoffer (2020), case-based teaching utilizes a combination of pedagogical elements: material, context, concepts, and method. The material is the medium used to present the case study, context the relevance to the curriculum, concepts the key theories or frameworks, and method the approach such as assignment or discussion (Hoffer 2020).

Furthermore, case studies typically include a decision-maker trying to solve a problem, a description of the problem, and supporting evidence to help make a decision regarding the problem (Boston University Center for Teaching & Learning, n.d.) But how to use case studies most effectively as an authentic learning method continues to be evaluated (Akbulut and Hill 2020). Akbulut and Hill (2020) propose an instructional model to help bridge some of the gaps in pedagogy.

Generally, the case study method in teaching uses a student-centered learning style making students more motivated to learn and engage with the course content (Çakmak and Akgün 2018). Radi Afsouran et al. (2018) discuss the theoretical implications of case studies and assert that case-method teaching has both advantages and disadvantages. Advantages include being a flexible and personalized way of teaching content.

In contrast, disadvantages can include finding appropriate and relatable case studies, educating instructors on how best to use case studies, and potential misunderstanding during class discussion (Radi Afsouran et al. 2018). Çakmak and Akgün (2018) also detail case study limitations such as challenges in managing debate, potential prejudices or biases from the instructor and/or students, and the time involved for instructors in preparing detailed case studies. As Rhodes, Wilson, and Rozell (2020) found, case-based learning might overwhelm less experienced students than a traditional lecture style of teaching might do.

However, case studies are ideal for demonstrating the complexity of the educational environment from teaching and learning to psychology and special education as well as administration and management (Nath 2005). There are several types of case studies depending on the scenario or behavior being addressed that spur discussion and debate.

Sykes and Bird (1992) surveyed the kinds of case studies used in education and broke them into five categories: textbook cases, casebooks, conversations and videotapes, subject-specific cases, and context-specific cases. Case studies have proven effective in enhancing student critical thinking (Sapeni and Said 2020), developing self-direction (Ameta, Tiwari, and Singh 2020), presenting real-world scenarios (Topperzer et al. 2021).

## SCHOOL LEADER PREPARATION PROGRAMS

The process to become a school superintendent varies from state to state and often includes obtaining an undergraduate degree, a master's or doctorate degree, and either a superintendent certification or an administrative services credential (Lynch 2019). To sit for the superintendent's certification or credential test, an individual must have either a master's degree or a specific number of years of teaching per state regulations is required (Lynch 2019). Superintendents need to have content expertise in curriculum and instruction, personnel management, communication, and relationship building (Antonucci 2012). The case studies in this book are about all of these topics and delve deeply into them.

The number of institutions granting degrees in educational administration increased by 72 percent this century (Perrone and Tucker 2019). Historically, university-based superintendent preparation programs have been criticized for being out of touch with the latest trends and needs in K-12 education (Lawrence 2008). It doesn't help that superintendent certification and eligibility requirements differ from state to state and frequently change. In addition, the pathway to becoming a school superintendent varies substantially depending on the educator's sex, race, and local employment setting, and age, sex, experience, education, and level of employment influence the likelihood of becoming a superintendent (Davis and Bowers 2019).

As a result, barriers continue to exist for those aspiring to become school superintendents. For example, the majority of school superintendents are White (68.8%), followed by Hispanic or Latino (13.2%) and Black or African American (11.0%), and only 7.5% are women (Zippia 2021). Despite this inequity, women generally have more classroom experience than their male counterparts (White 2021; Davis and Bowers 2019). This book seeks to level some of that playing field by giving future educational leaders the competencies to excel in their school environments. As a result most case studies here include data to inform the subject matter.

School superintendent preparation programs need updating and improvement to meet the needs of twenty-first-century schools and students (Sampson, Alford, and Marshall 2018). School leaders require new skills such as obtaining consensus, developing school culture, engaging all stakeholders, and analyzing data (Sampson, Alford, and Marshall 2018). School superintendents interviewed by Sampson, Alford, and Marshall (2018) recommended that preparatory programs provide internships, real-world experience, and simulated experiences. In addition, critics suggest school superintendent preparation programs include courses pertaining to school finance (Thiede 2020) and fundraising (Miller, Lu, and Gearhart 2020).

Despite existing school leader training programs, Yavuz, Madonia, and Abolafia (2018) found that after completing the first year of educational leadership training, only around half of the aspiring school leaders felt ready to develop highly qualified educators and lead adequately. In 2018, school leader preparation programs were recommended to be overhauled and redesigned (Wang et al. 2018). Following surveys and focus groups with stakeholders, Thiede (2020) concluded that faculty need to review their superintendent preparation programs to improve curriculum and instruction.

## CBL FOR SUPERINTENDENTS

A school superintendent must be many things to many people. Summers (2015) found that successful superintendents build trust, foster a culture of persistence and resilience, and encourage collaborative professional development. But the reality is school superintendents are accountable to several critical and unique stakeholders, including the school board, faculty, staff, parents, and students.

These school leaders faced unprecedented challenges during the COVID-19 pandemic, especially as they navigated the needs of a diverse community (Cash 2022). As a result of the pandemic and polarizing politics, superintendents are leaving the job at increased rates. Across the country, in 2021, the number of superintendents that left their job increased by 25 percent (Danahy 2022).

School superintendents base decisions on students' interests, perceptions of community acceptance, and advice from trusted confidantes (Hart 2018). Working through potential dilemmas using CBL is advantageous for school superintendents. Reviewing case studies gives superintendents the opportunity to determine how they would manage and mitigate similar crises (Hill 2016).

While some superintendents believe current programs are satisfactory, others have stipulated they would be better served by programs implementing more case studies, scenario-based instruction, and hands-on experiences (Antonucci 2012; Hozien 2019).

Courses for educational administration leaders are frequently comprised of experienced teachers preparing for a leadership position; therefore, using their experiences and CBL can evoke useful problem-solving discussions (Diamantes and Ovington 2003). CBL increases inclusion for diverse groups (Hoffer 2020). The School Superintendents Association even uses real-world situations in its Aspiring Superintendents Academy® to better prepare future superintendents.

CBL has been used in numerous professions to help train future lawyers, doctors, and entrepreneurs. It stands to reason that case study methodology would also benefit superintendents as they prepare to become school leaders. Using case studies allows superintendents to think strategically through potential problems without suffering the repercussions or fall out.

More school leadership programs should use case studies as a means of engaging students, fostering discussion, and making the curriculum applicable to the real world. Finally, all of the case studies in this book are aligned to the Professional Standards for Educational Leaders 2015.

# Guidelines for Using Case Studies and This Book in Class

Strategy tools allow you to better understand the different specific instructional issues in different situations and contexts. Using these tools will allow you the opportunity to demonstrate to your class that you fully understand the rationale of applying skill sets, which skill sets can be applied in different cases, and the limitations of some of the skills you have acquired in your principal preparation program in certain school contexts (Hozien 2017).

A framework one could use is the school district teacher observation model, value-added analysis, evaluation of a teacher's choice of strategy, identification of what the key implementation issues are, and analysis of how might problems of implementation be addressed; this might require you to apply the cultural context, due to the fact that the setting is rural, urban, or suburban, and the like, or contextual analysis. The issues being addressed in the case should become clear as you read and reread the entire case or parts of the case through several times (Christensen 1981).

Depending on the course objectives, the instructor may encourage students to follow a systematic approach to their analysis. Here is one way to approach the case studies in this book:

### STEPS IN ANALYZING A CASE STUDY

1. Identify the problem(s) posited by the case.
2. Analyze: Think through this material and justify why you have reached your conclusions.
3. Decide/decision-making: Identify a specific course of action for a school.
4. Application: Demonstrate your understanding.
5. Communication: Justify your decisions, course of action, and so on.

Usually students will work in groups in analyzing cases. This enhances their social skills through discussion, debate, and compromise. These are important skills in the world of work, where many people work on projects or set tasks as part of a team. Students might be expected to use case analysis as part of an assessment for school leaders. Students must therefore be able to summarize information succinctly and identify the most important points in the case, rather than merely regurgitating the case word for word (Schweitzer 2014).

In the most straightforward application, the presentation of the case study establishes a framework for analysis. It is helpful if the statement of the case provides enough information for the students to figure out solutions and then to identify how to apply those solutions in other similar situations. Instructors may choose to use several cases so that students can identify both the similarities and differences among the cases.

For each case study in this book, try to understand how to resolve the instructional leadership issue. This can be done by answering the questions at the end of each case study, or you can create a worksheet that looks like the one in the following (see table 1) for all the case studies, thereby creating a systematic analysis of the case studies. Depending on the course objectives, the instructor may encourage students to follow a systematic approach to their analysis (Hozien 2017).

Here is another example: ask the students to read each case study, give the students the worksheet in the following (see table 1, then place the students in groups, and have the student groups fill this worksheet out for each case study that is read. The instructor can do this at the end of every class or as a homework assignment. Then have the students discuss the case study in class. The student groups stand up and present the case study title and a brief synopsis of what the case study was about, then they answer the questions in the worksheet for each case study. Then the next group presents their case study, and so on.

**Table 1  Hozien's Case Study Analysis Worksheet**

Case study title
Brief synopsis
What issues are at stake here?
What should the principal do? (probe for why/justification)
If necessary, create a step-by-step short-term/long-term action plan
What would you hope your action/decision would accomplish?
What possible risks or "downsides" are there to your action/decision?

# PROFESSIONAL STANDARDS FOR EDUCATIONAL LEADERS IN 2015

A key component of this book is that all of the case studies are aligned with the Interstate School Leaders Licensure Consortium standards. The ISSLC practice/policy standards were replaced by Professional Standards for Educational Leaders (PSEL) as national standards in November 2015. These are standards approved by the National Policy Board for Education Administration (2015) geared toward all educational stakeholders. The case studies focus on the following:

Standard 1. Mission, Vision, and Core Values: Effective educational leaders develop, advocate, and enact a shared mission, vision, and core values of high-quality education and academic success and well-being of each student.
Standard 2. Ethics and Professional Norms: Effective educational leaders act ethically and according to professional norms to promote each student's academic success and well-being.
Standard 3. Equity and Cultural Responsiveness: Effective educational leaders strive for equity of educational opportunity and culturally responsive practices to promote each student's academic success and well-being.
Standard 4. Curriculum, Instruction, and Assessment: Effective educational leaders develop and support intellectually rigorous and coherent systems of curriculum, instruction, and assessment to promote each student's academic success and well-being.
Standard 5. Community of Care and Support for Students: Effective educational leaders cultivate an inclusive, caring, and supportive school community that promotes the academic success and well-being of each student.
Standard 6. Professional Capacity of School Personnel: Effective educational leaders develop the professional capacity and practice of school personnel to promote each student's academic success and well-being.
Standard 7. Professional Community for Teachers and Staff: Effective educational leaders foster a professional community of teachers and other professional staff to promote each student's academic success and well-being.
Standard 8. Meaningful Engagement of Families and Community: Effective educational leaders engage families and the community in meaningful, reciprocal, and mutually beneficial ways to promote each student's academic success and well-being.
Standard 9. Operations and Management: Effective educational leaders manage school operations and resources to promote each student's academic success and well-being.

Standard 10. School Improvement: Effective educational leaders act as agents of continuous improvement to promote each student's academic success and well-being.

## Case Study List by PSEL (2015) Standards

| Name | School District Type | Professional Standards for Educational Leaders or PSEL Standards |
| --- | --- | --- |
| Changing the Schools to Prison Pipeline | Suburban district | Ethics and Professional Norms 2c, e; Equity and Cultural Responsiveness 3c; Meaningful Engagement of Families and Community 8b |
| Low Income, High Expectations | Suburban district | Equity and Cultural Responsiveness 3c, Meaningful Engagement of Families and Community 8b, School Improvement 10a |
| Navigating Chartered Waters | Urban district | Community of Care and Support for Students 5c; Operations and Management 9d |
| What's in a Name? | Urban district | Ethics and Professional Norms 2d; Equity and Cultural Responsiveness 3a; Meaningful Engagement of families and Community 8b |
| Getting Them All across the Stage | Urban district | Curriculum, Instruction, and Assessment 4a; Community of Care and Support for Students 5e |
| Back to School | Suburban district | Curriculum, Instruction, and Assessment 4a; Community of Care and Support for Students 5e |
| Preparing for Diversity | Rural district | Equity and Cultural Responsiveness 3a, b, c |
| To V or Not to V | Urban district | Curriculum, Instruction, and Assessment 4d, e |
| Finances First | Urban district | Operations and Management 9d, h; Ethics and Professional Norms 3f |
| The Trauma-Informed Care Initiative | Suburban district | Professional Community for Teachers and Staff 7b; School Improvement 5a |
| How We've Always Done It | Rural district | Mission, Vision, and Core Values 1c; Equity and Cultural Responsiveness 3a, b |
| EBD in Pine Tree | Rural district | Equity and Cultural Responsiveness 3a, d; Community of Care and Support for Students 5e; School Improvement 10f |
| Case Study: Period Shaming | Suburban district | Equity and Cultural Responsiveness 3a, d; Community of Care and Support for Students 5e; |
| But They Have a Long Runway | Urban district | Professional Capacity of School Personnel 5a, c, d |
| More than Money | Rural district | Meaningful Engagement of Families and Community 8h, i |

| Name | School District Type | Professional Standards for Educational Leaders or PSEL Standards |
|---|---|---|
| Bonding with the Community | Suburban district | Meaningful Engagement of Families and Community 8g, h |
| Sure Shots | Suburban district | Professional Capacity of School Personnel 5g |
| Separate but Equal | Rural district | Community of Care and Support for Students 5b, c |
| Be My Guest | Rural district | Operations and Management 9d |
| Continuous Improvement Begins Here | Suburban district | School Improvement 10c, d |
| Reading between the Lines | Suburban district | School Improvement 10e |
| Every Child Matters | Suburban district | Ethics and Professional Norms 2b, c |
| Tomatoe, Tomato, What's Your Imago | Suburban district | Ethics and Professional Norms 2d, e |
| Zero Means Zero | Urban district | Mission, Vision, and Core Values 1b, c |
| A Personal Philosophy for the Public | Suburban district | Mission, Vision, and Core Values 1f, g |
| What's in a Grade? | Rural district | School Improvement 10d, e |
| Social Media Threat | Urban district | School Improvement 10h, i |
| White Flight | Suburban district | Mission, Vision, and Core Values 1b, e |
| Defining Moments | Urban district | Mission, Vision, and Core Values 1a |
| Evaluation Devaluation | Suburban School District | Professional Community for Teachers and Staff 7d, g; Professional Capacity of School Personnel 6a, e |

## Case Study Compiled by Standard

| Standard | Standard | All Case Study Names with These Standards |
|---|---|---|
| 1. Mission, Vision, and Core Values | Effective educational leaders develop, advocate, and enact a shared mission, vision, and core values of high-quality education and academic success and well-being of each student. | • The Trauma-Informed Care Initiative<br>• Zero Means Zero<br>• A Personal Philosophy for the Public<br>• White Flight<br>• Defining Moments |
| 2. Ethics and Professional Norms | Effective educational leaders act ethically and according to professional norms to promote each student's academic success and well-being. | • Changing the Schools to Prison Pipeline<br>• What's in a Name?<br>• Finances First<br>• Every Child Matters<br>• Tomatoe, Tomato, What's Your Imago |

*(Continued)*

(Continued)

| Standard | Standard | All Case Study Names with These Standards |
|---|---|---|
| 3. Equity and Cultural Responsiveness | Effective educational leaders strive for the equity of educational opportunity and culturally responsive practices to promote each student's academic success and well-being. | • Changing the Schools to Prison Pipeline<br>• Low Income, High Expectations<br>• What's in a Name?<br>• Preparing for Diversity<br>• How We've Always Done It?<br>• EBD in Pine Tree<br>• Period Shaming |
| 4. Curriculum, Instruction, and Assessment | Effective educational leaders develop and support intellectually rigorous and coherent systems of curriculum, instruction, and assessment to promote each student's academic success and well-being. | • Changing the Schools to Prison Pipeline<br>• Low Income, High Expectations<br>• What's in a Name?<br>• Preparing for Diversity<br>• How We've Always Done It<br>• EBD in Pine Tree<br>• To V or Not to V |
| 5. Community of Care and Support for Students | Effective educational leaders cultivate an inclusive, caring, and supportive school community that promotes the academic success and well-being of each student | • Navigating Chartered Waters<br>• Getting Them All across the Stage<br>• Back to School<br>• EBD in Pine Tree<br>• Separate but Equal<br>• Period Shaming |
| 6. Professional Capacity of School Personnel | Effective educational leaders develop the professional capacity and practice of school personnel to promote each student's academic success and well-being. | • But They Have a Long Runway<br>• Sure Shots<br>• Evaluation Devaluation |
| 7. Professional Community for Teachers and Staff | Effective educational leaders foster a professional community of teachers and other professional staff to promote each student's academic success and well-being. | • The Trauma-Informed Care Initiative<br>• Evaluation Devaluation |
| 8. Meaningful Engagement of Families and Community | Effective educational leaders engage families and the community in meaningful, reciprocal, and mutually beneficial ways to promote each student's academic success and well-being. | • Changing the Schools to Prison Pipeline<br>• Low Income, High Expectations<br>• What's in a Name?<br>• More than Money<br>• Bonding with the Community |

| Standard | Standard | All Case Study Names with These Standards |
|---|---|---|
| 9. Operations and Management | Effective educational leaders manage school operations and resources to promote each student's academic success and well-being. | • Navigating Chartered Waters<br>• Finances First<br>• Be My Guest |
| 10. School Improvement | Effective educational leaders manage school operations and resources to promote each student's academic success and well-being. | • Low Income, High Expectations<br>• The Trauma-Informed Care Initiative<br>• EBD in Pine Tree<br>• Continuous Improvement Begins Here<br>• Reading Between the Lines<br>• What's in a Grade?<br>• Social Media Threat |

*Note:* For ease of reference, these are the names of the case studies in this book with the national standards in the last column. Professional Standards for Educational Leaders retrieved from: http://www.npbea.org/wp-content/uploads/2017/06/Professional-Standards-for-Educational-Leaders_2015.pdf.

*Chapter 1*

# Our Mission, Vision, and Values Encompass Who We Are

At the core of the job of school superintendent is the mission and vision of who we are as a society and what we strive to cultivate: educational opportunity for all. The school district with the superintendent at the helm is committed to providing an environment that cultivates individual abilities, respects differences, and nurtures responsibility and cooperation.

School districts are a place dedicated to each of our children, devoted to our whole community, defined by our ideals, and providing the finest education. The school superintendent is proud to serve and support students.

Superintendents take seriously the educational values, opportunity, and responsibility they have to help serve the most valuable resource in our nation—our youth. It is the children of our school districts who inspire the quality of work and service superintendents strive to deliver.

In this chapter, the reader will find case studies that challenge the issues that we are grappling with on an everyday basis based on the mission, vision, and values we hold steadfastly to as a society.

## CASE STUDY: THE TRAUMA-INFORMED CARE INITIATIVE

Suburban district; Professional Community for Teachers and Staff 7b; School Improvement 5a

### Background

Dr. Hana Jackson has been the superintendent of schools at Columbia Valley School District for three years. During this time, the suburban district enrollment has grown by 8 percent each year. The district barely has earned the designation of "good" from the state education agency. It was nearly designated as "unacceptable," which is one rating below "good." The accountability designation is based on several factors, including national assessment scores, graduation rates, average GPA, attendance, college matriculation, and school safety. The highest rating for schools is "excellent," which is one level above "good."

During the past three years, Dr. Hana Jackson has noticed an upward trend in discipline referrals in her schools. Many of the incidents involve assault and other dangerous behaviors. Campus principals have reported that students are self-harming, having violent outbursts that result in property damage, and exhibiting highly aggressive behavior that damages school property. The principals have also reported that their teachers don't know how to handle discipline like this.

Dr. Hana Jackson is concerned about the impact this increase could have on school safety, and ultimately, instruction. There has also been a 4 percent increase in special education identification due to emotional and behavioral disorders.

**Issue**

Dr. Hana Jackson is worried that if the district rating slips below "good," the school board will not renew her contract. She has been tempted to tell the principals not to report some of the more violent behaviors in the data reporting system, but she wants the incidents of aggression and violence stopped.

Several administrators have had conversations with Dr. Hana Jackson about trauma-informed care. Clearly, more and more students have been exhibiting signs of emotional behavior disorders (EBD), and *DSM-5* testing of students confirms what the teachers are seeing.

They pointed out that the curriculum association has identified six areas that impact trauma-informed care:

- Safety
- Trustworthiness and transparency
- Peer support
- Collaboration and mutuality
- Empowerment and choice
- Cultural, historical, and gender issues.

The teachers insisted that by addressing each of these areas with their students, they can significantly reduce the behaviors. The principals want to empower their teachers to learn how to provide trauma-informed care for students in need.

Additionally, a study called "Disproportionality of Minority Students Identified with an Emotional/Behavioral Disorder" has identified the following teacher variables when dealing with EBD students (see tables 1.1 and 1.2):

Table 1.1. Hierarchal Linear Model with Competence as Outcome. Coefficients for Cross-Level Interaction of Teacher-Level Variables and Differences between African American and Caucasian Students

| Fixed Effect | Coefficient | Standard Ratio | T-ratio | Approx. df | p-Value |
|---|---|---|---|---|---|
| Teacher Age $B21^{ab}$ | −0.096 | 0.106 | −0.908 | 57 | 0.368 |
| Years of Experience $B22^{ab}$ | 0.035 | 0.159 | 0.222 | 57 | 0.825 |
| Management $B23^{ab}$ | −1.021 | 2.285 | −0.447 | 57 | 0.656 |
| External $B24^{ab}$ | −1.677 | 1.706 | −0.982 | 57 | 0.330 |
| Personal $B25^{ab}$ | 0.142 | 1.898 | 0.075 | 57 | 0.941 |
| Teacher Gender $B26^{ab}$ | 1.630 | 2.269 | 0.718 | 57 | 0.475 |
| Teacher Race/Ethnicity $B27^{ab}$ | −0.079 | 2.473 | −0.032 | 57 | 0.975 |

[a]This variable has been centered on its group mean.
[b]The residual parameter variance for the parameter has been set to zero.

Table 1.2. Hierarchal Linear Model with Competence as Outcome. Coefficients for Cross-Level Interaction of Teacher-Level Variables and Differences between Hispanic American and Caucasian Students

| Fixed Effect | Coefficient | Standard Ratio | T-ratio | Approx. df | p-Value |
|---|---|---|---|---|---|
| Teacher Age $B31^{ab}$ | −0.156 | 0.127 | −1.225 | 57 | 0.226 |
| Years of Experience $B32^{ab}$ | 0.178 | 0.219 | 0.811 | 57 | 0.421 |
| Management $B33^{ab}$ | −0.568 | 3.175 | −0.179 | 57 | 0.859 |
| External $B34^{ab}$ | −2.420 | 2.080 | −1.164 | 57 | 0.250 |
| Personal $B35^{ab}$ | 1.697 | 2.967 | 0.572 | 57 | 0.569 |
| Teacher Gender $B36^{ab}$ | −0.629 | 2.459 | −0.256 | 57 | 0.799 |
| Teacher Race/Ethnicity $B37^{ab}$ | −6.596 | 3.635 | −1.814 | 57 | 0.074 |

[a]This variable has been centered on its group mean.
[b]The residual parameter variance for the parameter has been set to zero.

Dr. Hana Jackson wants the campus administrators to handle discipline with zero tolerance. The principals have pointed out that 35 percent of variance in teacher-related internalizing problems lies at the teacher/classroom level and approximately 9 percent at the school level.

## Dilemma

The campus administrators feel that they have the data they need to make informed decisions about a trauma-informed care initiative and that should begin in the classrooms with teachers. The teachers know their students better than anyone, and teachers who have the skills to work with EBD students are more likely to effect positive change.

Dr. Hana Jackson, however, wants to see a top-down approach in which the principals come down hard on discipline problems. "After all, it's the same 5–10 percent that always ends up in your office. Deal with them, and everything else will be fine. Instruction will be fine. Behavior will be fine. And our rating will go up."

Dr. Hana Jackson must decide whether to encourage the teachers to experiment and innovate, or if she should take control of how the teachers respond to discipline problems in the classroom.

## Questions

1. What other data could help Dr. Hana Jackson with her decision?
2. Which factors have the greatest statistical significance?
3. How should the trauma-informed care initiative be implemented?
4. What is the role of the teachers in trauma-informed care? The campus administrators? The superintendent?
5. What should the principals do if Dr. Hana Jackson asks them to lie about the discipline data?
6. What other advice do you have for Dr. Hana Jackson?

## CASE STUDY: ZERO MEANS ZERO

Urban district; Mission, Vision, and Core Values 1b, c

### Background

The Emerson City School District established a zero-tolerance policy in 2001. The school board at the time had been concerned about continuous terrorist attacks after 9/11, and it made sense to them to come down hard against anyone bringing guns or knives to school.

The new policy seemed to be effective. In the first three years of its existence, the district saw a marked decline in incidents. By the fourth and fifth years that the zero-tolerance policy was in effect, Emerson City School District focused less on the effectiveness of their zero-tolerance policy and more on other issues in the district.

For one thing, student performance was declining. Fewer students were identified as Gifted and Talented, and enrollment in AP classes was down.

Overall, students were scoring 200 points less on their SAT exams than before the zero-tolerance policy was implemented.

Teachers complained that they didn't have enough time to teach. Constant interruptions came from the administration asking for data or other information, and they continued in class because of students who misbehaved and prevented others from getting any instruction.

Dr. Zakieh Stanford became the new Emerson City School District superintendent last year. Concerned about the poor academic performance, the superintendent requested data regarding the disciplinary actions taken during her first year in the district. She was aware of the teacher complaints, but she knew that the parents also had been complaining that their children got sent home all the time.

"How are kids supposed to learn if they're not in school?" posted one mom on social media. Her question generated a discussion that went viral.

The superintendent Dr. Zakieh Stanford reviewed the data.

## Issue

The data (see table 1.3) revealed that things were far worse than the superintendent thought. When looking at the disciplinary action taken against students, the superintendent Dr. Zakieh Stanford found a disturbing trend: Hispanic students were nearly twice as likely to suffer disciplinary action, and African American students were nearly three times as likely to be disciplined.

The disparity between White, Hispanic, and African American students continued to suffer, especially when considering the impact of the zero-tolerance policy that had been in place for nearly two decades.

## Dilemma

The superintendent Dr. Zakieh Stanford felt as though Emerson City School District was building a school to prison pipeline instead of providing the solid academic foundation students needed and deserved. No wonder the parents complained about the school policies, especially the zero-tolerance policy.

It was obvious that White students seemed to be getting preferential treatment. More of them were enrolled in AP courses, and they were more likely to be identified as GT and less likely to need special education services or Section 504 support. The superintendent had to get rid of the zero-tolerance policy that had been part of the district's philosophy for so long.

**Table 1.3. Student Data.**

| Discipline Steps Taken | Black Male | Black Female | Hispanic Male | Hispanic Female | White Male | White Female |
|---|---|---|---|---|---|---|
| Overall Students Identified for Disciplinary Action | 378 | 274 | 256 | 225 | 137 | 82 |
| Students without Disabilities | 201 | 180 | 194 | 163 | 115 | 69 |
| Students with Disabilities Served under IDEA | 120 | 73 | 54 | 40 | 14 | 9 |
| Students with Disabilities Served under Section 504 | 37 | 21 | 11 | 22 | 8 | 4 |
| Students Who Received Corporal Punishment | 0 | 0 | 0 | 0 | 0 | 0 |
| Students Who Received Out-of-School Suspension | 298 | 233 | 207 | 198 | 27 | 6 |
| Students Who Received an Expulsion | 54 | 23 | 41 | 19 | 4 | 1 |
| Students without Disabilities Who Received an Expulsion under Zero-Tolerance Policies | 52 | 19 | 36 | 13 | 2 | 0 |
| Students with Disabilities Who Received an Expulsion under Zero-Tolerance Policies | 29 | 17 | 21 | 14 | 0 | 0 |
| Students without Disabilities Transferred to an Alternative School for Disciplinary Reasons | 121 | 92 | 59 | 26 | 13 | 5 |
| Students with Disabilities Transferred to an Alternative School for Disciplinary Reasons | 44 | 29 | 38 | 25 | 3 | 0 |
| Students without Disabilities Who Were Referred to a Law Enforcement Agency or Official | 117 | 100 | 89 | 74 | 21 | 12 |
| Students with Disabilities Who Were Referred to a Law Enforcement Agency or Official | 64 | 42 | 57 | 31 | 7 | 1 |
| Students without Disabilities Who Received a School-Related Arrest | 79 | 65 | 62 | 54 | 6 | 0 |
| Students with Disabilities Who Received a School-Related Arrest | 36 | 35 | 31 | 22 | 3 | 0 |
| Gifted and Talented Student Enrollment | 11 | 23 | 27 | 45 | 48 | 54 |
| Students Enrolled in at least One AP Course | 2 | 3 | 4 | 7 | 13 | 17 |

## Questions

1. What does the data reveal about students with disabilities and without disabilities?
2. What conjectures can you make about the district's corporal punishment policy?
3. What other data does the superintendent need?
4. What steps would you recommend that the superintendent take to revise the zero-tolerance policy at Emerson City School District?
5. Who should be involved in the decision-making process, and why?

## CASE STUDY: A PERSONAL PHILOSOPHY FOR THE PUBLIC

Suburban district; Mission, Vision, and Core Values 1f, g

### Background

It was already January, and once again Superintendent Ismail Fitzpatrick was working on his annual evaluation. The data he collected spanned the past four years and represented his work in the Cecil H. Green Public School District (see Figure 1.1).

| School Metric | 2016 | 2017 | 2018 | 2019 |
|---|---|---|---|---|
| **Academics** | | | | |
| Student achievement in math | 319 | 317 | 326 | 320 |
| Student achievement in reading | 358 | 365 | 383 | 391 |
| Student growth in math (+) | 21 | 19 | 26 | 22 |
| Student growth in reading (+) | 33 | 37 | 45 | 51 |
| **Attendance** | | | | |
| Student | 85 | 88 | 92 | 93 |
| Employee | 77 | 86 | 85 | 89 |
| **Evaluations** | | | | |
| % Completed on time | 100 | 100 | 100 | 99 |
| % Incomplete, or not completed on time | 0 | 0 | 0 | 1 |
| **Feedback** | | | | |
| Rating from community (1–10) | 6.8 | 7.2 | 7.4 | 8.5 |
| Rating from employees (1–10) | 9.3 | 8.9 | 9.1 | 6.5 |
| Rating from board (1–10) | 8.5 | 8.3 | 8.9 | 9.1 |

**Figure 1.1.** Ismail Fitzpatrick's Evaluation Data

Cecil Green is a small suburban district that is made up of a close-knit community. The district has no residence requirement for their teachers because affordable housing is difficult to find. Many of the teachers live in nearby towns and cities that offer more amenities than Cecil Green. Even the superintendent had had difficulty finding appropriate housing for his family, but he finally found a home that would fit his family's needs. It was two miles outside the district's boundaries, but the board had no issue with the location.

Superintendent Ismail Fitzpatrick's children attended a different school district than where he worked. The superintendent discovered that he and his wife preferred that arrangement because he didn't have to worry about his children getting preferential treatment because they were the superintendent's kids.

He was relieved that they didn't attend Cecil Green because frankly, the math performance wasn't what he had hoped it would be. The elementary schools always performed well, and so did the sixth and seventh graders. Eighth-grade scores, however, always seemed to fall like they were going over a cliff. It wasn't until the 10th grade that math scores began to come back up. He wasn't sure if it was the curriculum, the teacher skill set, or teenage hormones that were a problem. Superintendent Ismail Fitzpatrick wished he didn't have to aggregate those two years in his summary data.

As he prepared his evaluation, Superintendent Ismail Fitzpatrick glanced over the data again. The evaluation was weighted. Around 30 percent of the annual evaluation would be based on performance over the previous three years. Around 50 percent of the evaluation would come from the current year's performance. The remaining 20 percent came from the superintendent's ability to:

- work ethically
- establish a mission and vision for the district
- create a positive work environment

## Issue

Superintendent Ismail Fitzpatrick believed that good things came to those who worked for them. He felt like he demonstrated a strong work ethic, and others should do the same.

In his mind, that same work ethic would help students in the classroom. Rather than complain that they don't understand something, students should buckle down and do the assignments. The same thing was true for teachers. Rather than whine that the math program wasn't working, they should work and find supplemental materials that supported their instruction.

"How hard is it to find ways to work around problems? You get a paycheck; do your job," said Fitzpatrick. The problem is that the superintendent posted this comment on his social media page.

## Dilemma

It didn't take long for the teachers to find the superintendent's post. They began sharing his comments, along with several others that he had made.

The school board has requested that in addition to providing an evaluation summary based on data, Superintendent Ismail Fitzpatrick revise his personal mission statement, aligning it more closely with the goals of the district. They planned to share it on the district webpage.

The mission statement read,

> My mission is to provide every student in Cecil H. Green a quality education based on best practices in education—for every subject in every grade. In addition, I believe in nurturing the careers of our teachers and giving them all the support, they need.

When he turned in the personal mission statement, the board president said, "I don't think you believe any of this."

## Questions

1. The evaluation data include both student growth and student achievement. Why should both measures be part of the evaluation?
2. What should the superintendent do about the math scores?
3. Which areas of the evaluation would you ask the superintendent to work on first and why?
4. The school board has given the superintendent a high rating. Should the board change its evaluation of the superintendent? Why or why not?
5. If the data in this case were yours, what would your personal mission statement be?

## CASE STUDY: WHITE FLIGHT

Suburban district; Mission, Vision, and Core Values 1b, e

## Background

Ford School District was one of several schools in a suburban area of the state. In two years' time the district had seen a significant district drop in the enrollment of White students. As more Hispanic and African American students were moving into Ford, White families were either moving out or withdrawing their children from the Ford schools and transferring them to nearby schools.

The enrollment trends are shown in figure 1.2.

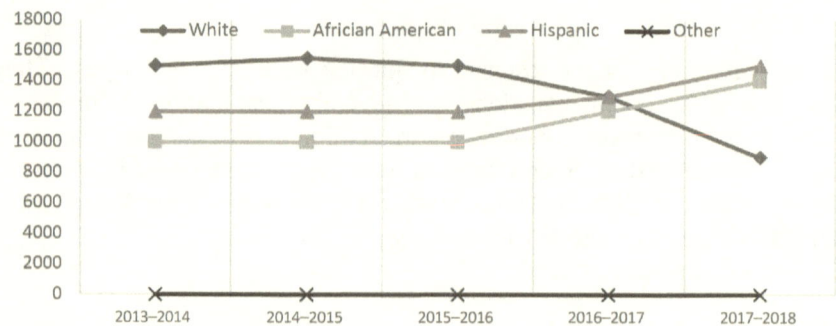

Figure 1.2.  **Enrollment Trends**

Parents cited many reasons for their decision. Including a general unhappiness with the schools in Ford or how the neighborhoods seemed to be changing, and not for the better. They cited a rise in crime, especially burglaries, and they wondered how safe the school would be.

The superintendent, Dr. Ahmad Carmichael, noticed other changes in the Ford schools, including the following:

- Bullying has increased 58 percent in two years' time.
- GPAs have increased from 3.1 to 3.2
- The number of qualified teachers in the district has decreased by 5 percent, and 65 percent of the faculty have 0–5 years of teaching experience.
- Scores on college entrance exams have decreased by 100 points.
- Enrollment in AP classes has declined by 25 percent.
- Enrollment in remedial classes has increased by 20 percent.
- Dual enrollment in high school and college course has decreased from 37 percent to 12 percent.
- Suspensions and expulsions have increased by 17 percent, and of those students referred for disciplinary action, 48 percent were African American, 32 percent were Hispanic, and 20 percent were White.
- Last year, the high school reported three incidents of weapons on campus, and when a riot broke out, the police had to be called.

In addition, the district was losing money every time a student transferred to another district. Every transfer student cost the district $8,735 in revenue.

**Issue**

Superintendent Ahmad Carmichael was well aware that White flight was causing the district to lose money. In addition, the Ford district now had to spend more money on remedial courses and less on AP and advanced coursework. Fewer students were college-bound because they did not have the scores for entrance into higher learning, nor did they have the academic rigor.

White flight was draining the district dry, and it had to be stopped.

## Dilemma

The superintendent Dr. Ahmad Carmichael issued a directive that no student transfers would be approved. District personnel were coached to hold meetings with the concerned parents, listen to the reasons given for the transfer, and forward all paperwork to his office where it would be approved or denied.

No White student transfers were approved. Students of color, however, were approved for transfer. They constituted 1 percent of all transfer requests.

## Questions

1. What do the data trends reveal?
2. Can a superintendent prevent students from transferring to another school district?
3. How did the superintendent prevent students from being successful?
4. What data measures increased? Why do you think that is?
5. What could be done to meet the needs of White students, so they don't enroll in other districts?
6. What challenges would you address first, and why?

## CASE STUDY: DEFINING MOMENTS

Urban district; Mission, Vision, and Core Values 1a

## Background

Serene Fielding, J.D. is the new superintendent at Hardwell Public Schools, which is an inner-city school district.

The superintendent knew the law inside and out, and when she took the job as the district leader after having served as the district lawyer, she knew that she would have to improve student achievement. Last year, student growth decreased 10 points in reading and 14 points in math.

Other challenges included a 28 percent increase in out-of-school suspensions for minority students. Around 65% of the suspensions were the result of classroom behaviors, another 15 percent were because of behaviors in the hallways and other common areas of the schools. The last 20 percent occurred while riding school transportation.

There had been seventeen arrests made on the campuses. Nine of the arrests were for assault, six for drugs, and three for weapons, including one gun. All seventeen students were expelled.

Other challenges in the district included having an outdated curriculum, old and battered textbooks, and the teacher requests for continued professional development outside the district were repeatedly denied. In spite of not being encouraged to grow professionally, the teachers congratulated themselves for doing a good job despite the challenges they faced.

The superintendent Dr. Serene Fielding had tons of work ahead of her. What had been working before no longer was effective for students or their teachers. The district needed a new mission and vision.

Every parent, teacher, student, and school board member received a survey asking for their input about district issues. Even some of the community members received a survey. The superintendent compiled all the results into a single chart (see figure 1.3).

The survey included an area for comments, some of which included:

- We're doing the best we can with virtually nothing and no support.
- Students deserve better, and so do we.
- This district is excellent.
- I hate the cafeteria food.
- I haven't learned anything new in years.
- My kids aren't getting what they need.

## Issue

With the survey results back, Superintendent Serene met with her cabinet to review the collected data and strategize ways to improve education in the district.

The cabinet identified two major areas of need:

- safe schools
- professional development

It was obvious to everyone in the meeting that school safety had to be a priority. Unless they had a firm grasp on classroom management, the schools

*Our Mission, Vision, and Values Encompass Who We Are* 13

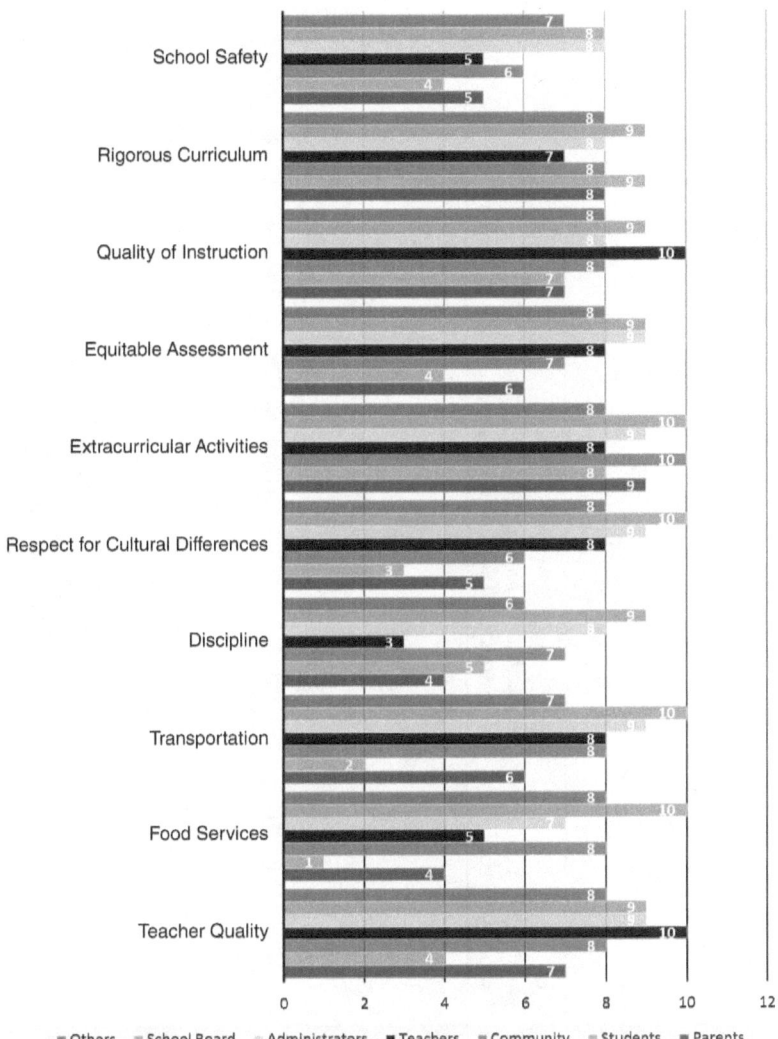

**Figure 1.3. Survey Results for Hardwell Public Schools**

would continue to be unsafe. Their current discipline practices clearly weren't working.

To help teachers with classroom management techniques, the district would have to encourage participation in professional development in dealing with student behaviors and improving the quality of the curriculum and instruction.

| | School Safety | Rigorous Curriculum | Quality of Instruction | Equitable Assessment | Extracurricular Activities | Respect for cultural Differences | Discipline | Transportation | Food Services | Teacher Quality |
|---|---|---|---|---|---|---|---|---|---|---|
| **Parents** | 5 | 8 | 7 | 6 | 9 | 5 | 4 | 6 | 4 | 7 |
| **Students** | 4 | 9 | 7 | 4 | 8 | 3 | 5 | 2 | 1 | 4 |
| **Community** | 6 | 8 | 8 | 7 | 10 | 6 | 7 | 8 | 8 | 8 |
| **Teachers** | 5 | 7 | 10 | 8 | 8 | 8 | 3 | 8 | 5 | 10 |
| **Administrators** | 8 | 8 | 8 | 9 | 9 | 9 | 8 | 9 | 7 | 9 |
| **School Board** | 8 | 9 | 9 | 9 | 10 | 10 | 9 | 10 | 10 | 9 |
| **Others** | 7 | 8 | 8 | 8 | 8 | 8 | 6 | 7 | 8 | 8 |

## Dilemma

Superintendent Serene took her cabinet's recommendations seriously; she completely agreed with their analysis. Eventually, the district would have to revise its mission and vision. These goals would need board approval.

When Superintendent Serene discussed the cabinet's work with the school board, she was met with resistance. The school board felt as though the district was doing fine. They weren't interested in making any drastic changes, as they called them.

If the superintendent could do anything to help the district be better, it would be to keep teachers around longer.

## Questions

1. Which stakeholders are the most critical of the school district? Which are the most complimentary?
2. What does the survey data reveal about the school board's attitudes?
3. Do you agree with the priorities identified by the superintendent and her cabinet? Why or why not?
4. How can the district retain good teachers?
5. How could the superintendent convince the board to let her intervene and make changes in the district's programs?

*Chapter 2*

# Coming to Terms with Ethics in Our Profession

When interviewing and shadowing school superintendents, ethics is the number one topic that comes up over and over again. Having a strong moral compass and identifying those ethics and not wavering from those ethics are what determine the longevity of who stays in that position. The purpose of this case study book is to explore the decision-making processes of public school superintendents and to identify those factors that influenced decision-making.

Each day school leaders are faced with difficult dilemmas that call for them to act quickly, but in a just manner (Noppe et al. 2013). Yet, in accordance with making such decisions, there is a call on the character based on the school leader's judgment (Jacobs and Kritsonis 2007). This call on character is a focus of all stakeholders including the school board, students, parents, staff, and community members, mainly because as school leaders make decisions, their morals should be just as involved with the rational thinking part of the problem. That is, decisions should be made morally and ethically with regard to the best interest of their stakeholders.

Ethical leadership embodies ideals that any person in a leadership position should not neglect (Gamson 2004). For school superintendents, such practices are essential when it comes to the policies or reforms that are brought forth to be implemented in their respective districts and state. As pressure mounts from society, policy makers, other leaders, stakeholders, and in general, a need for change, school leaders must not be neglectful in their use of "practitioner-based ethic to critique" (Gamson 2004). The ethic of critique as taken from Starratt (1991) suggests the routine practice of leaders should include a constant reflection on the current policies and procedures in order to identify any injustices. From this one concept alone, the necessity for school leaders to actively practice ethical leadership is just one of many important means to achieve success in schools across the United States. Let's take a look at the case studies in this chapter and see how one might resolve issues related to ethics in the profession.

## CASE STUDY: CHANGING THE SCHOOLS TO PRISON PIPELINE

Suburban district; Ethics and Professional Norms 2c, e; Equity and Cultural Responsiveness 3c; Meaningful Engagement of Families and Community 8b

### Background

Dr. Isra Styles is the superintendent of the Widener District, where she oversees a suburban district serving 36,000 students in grades Pre-K through 12. Five high schools prepare students for graduation and their careers/college beyond, and the campuses serve approximately 2,000 students each. There are four counselors and five police officers at each school, in addition to the instructional and support staff.

The district is 30 percent Black, 30 percent Hispanic, and 30 percent White. Asian students make up the other 10 percent of the population. Even though the school budget has been limited, and state/federal accountability demands high, Dr. Isra Styles has done what she thought was necessary to serve student needs. In the past two years, her human resources department has hired more teachers of color. Campus teachers worked during the summer months to rewrite the curriculum, making it more relevant to student culture and interests.

Dr. Isra Styles notes that she has been responsive to student behavior. In the past two years, acts of vandalism increased by 18 percent. Student absenteeism increased by 25 percent. Student aggression is up by 12 percent, drug abuse by 28 percent, and general violations of the student code of conduct skyrocketed to 52 percent. Last year, Dr. Isra Styles advocated for an increase of school police officers at each of the high school campuses, and the school board agreed to add the additional positions to the district.

Jamala was one of 547 arrestees this academic year. It was the third time she was arrested for vandalizing the girls' restroom. Jamala, who had just broken up with her boyfriend, was caught writing graffiti on the wall near the washbasin:

Drip, tears,
Like an old faucet
Like a cold love
I'm gonna cross it
Off my fears . . .

That was all she had written before one of the female police officers walked in, saw the graffiti and arrested Jamala.

### Issue

Jamala's arrest wasn't unusual. In the Widener District, Black students, especially girls, were arrested or given referrals to law enforcement twice as often as Hispanic students and three times as White students. This pattern was nearly identical to the national trends collected by the United States Department of Justice (see figures 2.1 and 2.2 and table 2.1).

These referrals and arrests make students of color far more likely to experience alienation and drop out of school. Parents feel that their children need counselors, not cops. The students themselves have reported that it is difficult getting to see their counselor because the counseling staff is focused on helping with assessments and getting "those kids" into college. There's no time to talk about the emotional, social, and physical issues teens experience.

In the past few months, Dr. Isra Styles's leadership has come into question. Citing national research, parents feel that the superintendent is not aware of the school-to-prison pipeline's current research. They have noted an inadequate student-to-counselor ratio, as seen in the following chart (see table 2.2 and figure 2.3).

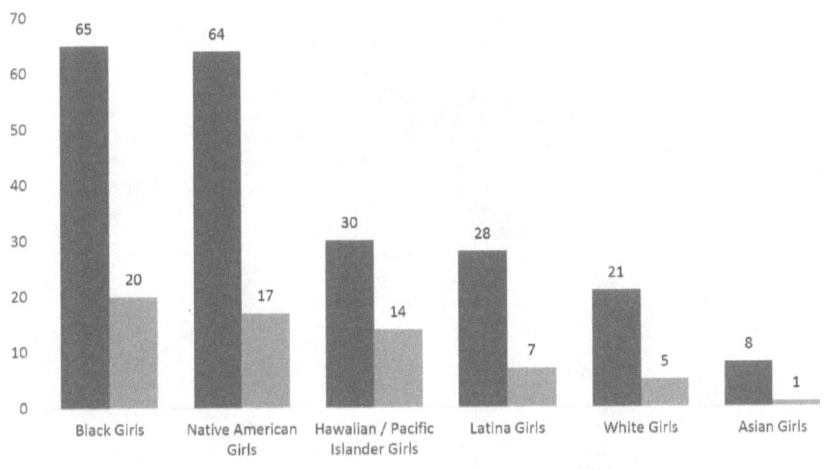

**Figure 2.1. School Connections and Referrals to Law Enforcement for Girls**

**Table 2.1. Black Girls Are Four Times More Likely to Be Arrested in School than White Girls Nationally.**

| 0–1 × as Likely to be Arrested as White Girls | 2–3 × as Likely to be Arrested as White Girls | 4–5 × as Likely to be Arrested as White Girls | 6–7 × as Likely to be Arrested as White Girls | 8+ × as Likely to be Arrested as White Girls |
|---|---|---|---|---|
| Idaho | Arizona | Kansas | California | West Virginia |
| Alaska | Arkansas | Illinois | Connecticut | Iowa |
| Maine | Colorado | Massachusetts | Kentucky | Michigan |
| Montana | Delaware | Minnesota | Louisiana | North Carolina |
| Nebraska | Florida | New Jersey | North Dakota | |
| Nevada | Georgia | Pennsylvania | Rhode Island | |
| Oregon | Hawaii | Texas | Wisconsin | |
| South Dakota | Indiana | Vermont | New Hampshire | |
| Utah | Maryland | Tennessee | | |
| Washington | Mississippi | Alabama | | |
| Wyoming | Missouri | | | |
| | New Mexico | | | |
| | New York | | | |
| | Ohio | | | |
| | Oklahoma | | | |
| | South Carolina | | | |
| | Tennessee | | | |
| | Virginia | | | |

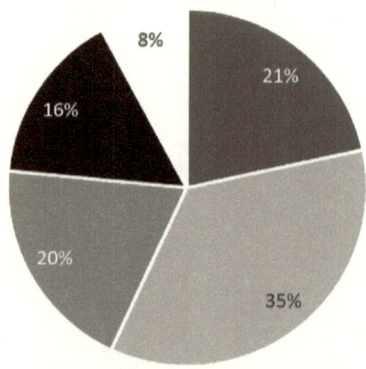

- 0–1x as likely to be arrested as White Girls
- 2–3x as likely to be arrested as White Girls
- 4–5x as likely to be arrrested as White Girls
- 6–7x as likely to be arrested as White Girls
  8+x as likely to be arrested as White Girls

**Figure 2.2. Black Girls' Arrest Rates Compared to White Girls' Arrest Rates.** *Note:* Each shade represents the states listed in table 2.1.

**Table 2.2. Forty-Seven States and D.C. Don't Meet the Recommended Student-to-Counselor Ratio.**

| Not Meeting Recommended Ratio | Meeting Recommended Ratio |
| --- | --- |
| Alabama | New Hampshire |
| Alaska | Vermont |
| Arizona | Montana |
| Arkansas | |
| California | |
| Colorado | |
| Connecticut | |
| Delaware | |
| Florida | |
| Georgia | |
| Hawaii | |
| Idaho | |
| Illinois | |
| Indiana | |
| Iowa | |
| Kansas | |
| Kentucky | |
| Louisiana | |
| Maine | |
| Maryland | |
| Massachusetts | |
| Michigan | |
| Minnesota | |
| Mississippi | |
| Missouri | |
| Nebraska | |
| Nevada | |
| New Jersey | |
| New Mexico | |
| New York | |
| North Carolina | |
| North Dakota | |
| Ohio | |
| Oklahoma | |
| Oregon | |
| Pennsylvania | |
| Rhode Island | |
| South Carolina | |
| South Dakota | |
| Tennessee | |
| Texas | |
| Utah | |
| Virginia | |
| Washington | |
| West Virginia | |
| Wisconsin | |
| Wyoming | |

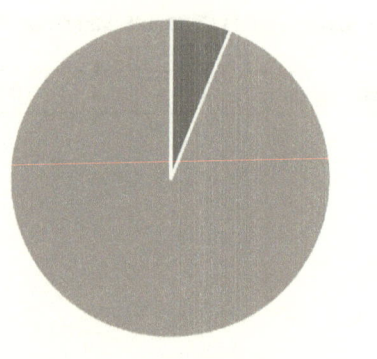

■ Meeting Recommended Ratio    ■ Not Meeting Recommended Ratio

**Figure 2.3. U.S. State Student-to-Counselor Ratio**

Superintendent Dr. Isra Styles has already used more than her budgeted resources to increase police supervision on each of the five high schools in her district. There's no way to increase the number of counselors on staff. However, the parents and the community are demanding that Dr. Isra Styles meet the demands of the Black Lives Matter (BLM) movement:

- End zero tolerance;
- Mandate Black history and ethnic studies;
- Hire more Black teachers; and especially,
- Fund counselors, not cops.

### Dilemma

Parent and community involvement in the BLM movement has brought schools into focus. Community frustration with school arrests has served as the catalyst for action. Educating all students on BLM issues is a priority. Parents have pointed out that they need help educating their children, not preventing them from obtaining it. They specifically want more counselors at each of the high school and fewer police officers. They want the school-to-prison pipeline stopped.

Many of the students refuse to show respect to the counselors or police officers. Referrals and getting arrested means little to them.

### Questions

1. What other data do you recommend that Dr. Isra Styles consider before making staffing decisions?
2. If Dr. Isra Styles is going to add counselors to the staff at each high school, when should she make the change?

3. What advice would you give Dr. Isra Styles regarding reducing the number of police officers at each campus?
4. A change in staffing patterns might not be the only change the Widener District needs. What supporting issues should the district consider?
5. Should the superintendent organize a parent recommendation committee to assist with staffing decisions? Why or why not?
6. Does Dr. Isra Styles's race and ethnicity matter in this situation? Why or why not?

## CASE STUDY: WHAT'S IN A NAME?

Urban district; Ethics and Professional Norms 2d; Equity and Cultural Responsiveness 3a; Meaningful Engagement of families and Community 8b

### Background

City District #2 has a long legacy of educating students. After more than a century of providing instruction in its schools, the district finds itself on the brink of change.

The school district has always considered itself responsive yet traditional. Each school board valued community leaders' contributions, and the two dozen district campuses were named after prominent citizens in the community. These people were instrumental in shaping the vision of what this area of the city would evolve into. Currently, the campuses bear the names of twenty-one White people and three Latino people. No campuses have been named after a Black person. Seventeen campuses are named after men, and seven after women.

Approximately 62 percent of the community population is White, 20 percent is Hispanic/Latino, 13 percent is Black, and 5 percent is Asian. These percentages have remained consistent throughout the twentieth century and into the first two decades of the twenty-first century.

The numbers mirror the population trends by race and ethnicity predicted by the U.S. government. The government expects a declining White population by the year 2060 (see table 2.3).

### Issue

The advent of BTM in the past few years has helped the Black community find the courage to speak up and make demands they want to be met. On a national level, these demands include:

1. End the war on Black people.
2. Reparations for past and continuing harms. (Reparations)

**Table 2.3. Population by Race and Ethnicity: Projections 2030 to 2060, in Thousands. The Non-Hispanic White Population is Projected to Shrink by Nearly 19 Million People by 2060.**

| Characteristics | Population 2016 | | Population 2030 | | Population 2060 | | Change from 2016 to 2060 | |
|---|---|---|---|---|---|---|---|---|
| | Number | Percentage | Number | Percentage | Number | Percentage | Number | Percentage |
| Total Population | 323,128 | 10 | 355,101 | 10 | 404,483 | 10 | 51,355 | 25 |
| One Race | | | | | | | | |
| White | 248,503 | 76.9 | 263,453 | 74.2 | 275,014 | 68 | 26,511 | 10.7 |
| Non-Hispanic White | 197,970 | 61.3 | 197,992 | 55.8 | 179,162 | 44.3 | −18,808 | −9.5 |
| Black or African American | 43,001 | 13.3 | 49,009 | 13.8 | 60,690 | 15 | 17,689 | 41.1 |
| American Indian and Alaska Native | 4,055 | 1.3 | 4,663 | 1.3 | 5,583 | 1.4 | 1,528 | 37.7 |
| Asian | 18,319 | 5.7 | 24,394 | 6.9 | 38,815 | 9.1 | 18,496 | 101 |
| Native Hawaiian and other Pacific Islander | 771 | 0.2 | 913 | 0.4 | 1.125 | 0.3 | 354 | 45.9 |
| Two or More Races | 8,480 | 2.6 | 12,669 | 3.6 | 25,255 | 6.2 | 16,775 | 197.8 |
| Hispanic | 57,470 | 17.8 | 74,807 | 21.1 | 111,216 | 27.5 | 53,746 | 93.5 |

3. Divestment from the institutions that criminalize, cage, and harm black people; and investment in the education, health, and safety of black people. (Invest-Divest)
4. Economic justice for all and a reconstruction of the economy to ensure our communities have collective ownership, not merely access. (Economic justice)
5. Community control of the laws, institutions, and policies that most impact us. (Community control)
6. Independent Black political power and Black self-determination in all areas of society. (Political power)

Locally, many businesses are displaying signs showing support for BLM. Flags and shirts have become prominent. The Black community leaders in Quincy City District have requested a meeting with superintendent Dr. Edward Brown. The community-BLM coalition is demanding that the school district change the names of at least half of the schools. They want the schools renamed after national Black leaders.

## Dilemma

Dr. Brown has not yet met with the BLM leaders. He's been evasive, telling his secretary to take messages and not commit to a meeting on his behalf just yet. He wanted first to gather data. Dr. Brown asked for the breakdown of the race and ethnicity of the district's students. Not surprisingly, the data were similar to data collected nationally (see figure 2.4). If the projections hold true, City District #2 would also see an eventual decline among White

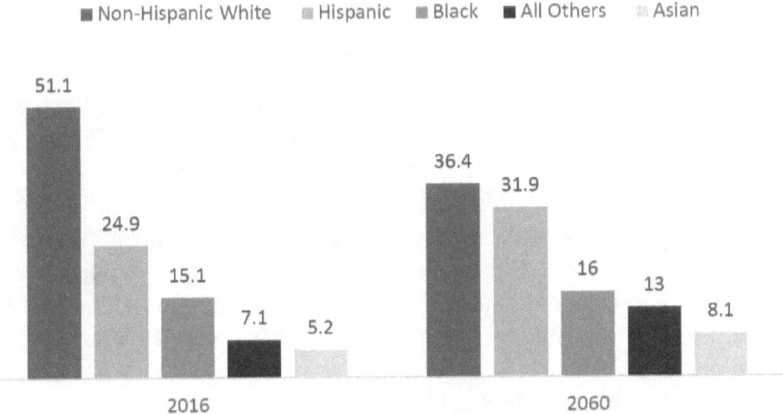

**Figure 2.4. Racial and Ethnic Composition: Children under Eighteen Years Old**

students and a significant increase in Hispanic students by 2060. There will also be a considerable increase in the number of schools the district will need.

Dr. Brown must meet with the BLM community leaders soon. What should he tell them about their request to change at least half of the schools' names?

Additionally, the campus administrators have called with concerns about the BLM movement. Students want to stage a protest and wear BLM shirts to school.

## Questions

1. What advice would you give Dr. Brown regarding the meeting with the BLM community activists?
2. Does race and ethnicity representation matter for the make-up school board? Why or why not?
3. Should the student be allowed to wear BLM shirts to school and stage a protest?
4. Should Dr. Brown encourage the community BLM activists to become more active in campus activities? Why or why not?
5. Should Dr. Brown encourage BLM activists to run for school board? Why or why not?
6. Should the district rename the schools? Why or why not?

## CASE STUDY: FINANCES FIRST

Urban district; Operations and Management 9d, h; Ethics and Professional Norms 3f

### Background

After a series of financial errors that included acts of omission as well as acts of commission, The Teneforth School District hired a new female superintendent to take the reins of the mid-sized urban school district.

Upon accepting the position and moving into the office, Dr. Maram Clifford had to make sense of the financial mess in which the former superintendent had left the district. She understood that whatever she did, her efforts were not going to be appreciated. "Here we go," she thought. Her new administrative assistant was full of gossip about what had happened and who had been involved, but Dr. Maram Clifford wasn't interested in gossip; she was interested in increased student achievement.

The courts had already determined wrongdoing, and eight indicted district employees were now serving time in jail for crimes ranging from theft to misappropriation of funds.

Dr. Maram Clifford was interested in getting the campuses and the Teneforth School District back on the right fiscal accountability track.

The state recognized fiscal responsibility as a significant part of the accountability arena. School districts that were unable to manage their money were monitored closely, and if need be, taken over by the state agency or closed.

Accountability indicators for fiscal responsibility included:

- annual results and recommendations from an external auditor
- accuracy in reporting
- the number of accounts paid in thirty/sixty/ninety days
- whether the district maintained a two- or three-month payroll reserve
- spending by program and account, and
- the amount of debt carried by the district compared to its cash reserves.

All districts are required to hold an annual meeting explaining their ability to meet these standards. Teneforth School District had been awarded a rating of Bronze Standard. One middle school and one charter school within the district had each earned a rating of No Confidence. The middle school had a Silver Standard rating the year before, and last year was the charter school's first year of operation. There was no public meeting held the prior two years regarding fiscal responsibility and transparency.

A comparative analysis of financial rating is given in the following (see table 2.4):

Table 2.4. Finance Ratings for the State, Charters, and Teneforth School District

| Rating | Districts | % | Charters | % | Total | % | Teneforth Campuses | % |
|---|---|---|---|---|---|---|---|---|
| Gold Standard | 81 | 84.83% | 123 | 74.10% | 990 | 83.33% | 7 | 43.75% |
| Silver Standard | 12 | 11.25% | 24 | 14.46% | 139 | 11.70% | 5 | 31.25% |
| Bronze Standard | 4 | 4.0% | 16 | 9.64% | 51 | 4.30% | 4 | 25.0% |
| No Confidence | 2 | 2.0% | 3 | 1.81% | 8 | 0.67% | 2 | 12.5% |
| Total | 100 | 100.00% | 166 | 100.00% | 1188 | 100.00% | 16 | 100.00% |

A closer inspection revealed the following information (see table 2.5):

Table 2.5. Fiscal Compliance for Teneforth District

| Indicator | District Response |
|---|---|
| Annual Results and Recommendations from an External Auditor | No |
| Accuracy in Reporting | No |
| The Number of Accounts Paid in Thirty/Sixty/Ninety Days | 59%/30%/11% |
| Whether the District Maintained a Two- or Three-Month Payroll Reserve | Yes |
| Spending by Program and Account | Usually |
| The Amount of Debt Carried by the District Compared to Its Cash Reserves | No data found |

## Issue

Teneforth School District has been in the news for its fiscal irresponsibility. Eight administrative employees are serving time in jail for illegal practices regarding operating the school budgets. The charges included theft, embezzlement, and failure to meet Open Records standards.

The former superintendent hired a family member to serve as the outside accounting firm that would provide the audits confirming the district's integrity.

The new superintendent has just taken over the office and is reviewing fiscal practices that have been adopted in the district. Already two of the Teneforth campuses have received a rating of "No Confidence," and it appears that others may be headed down the same path. A district with a rating of "No Confidence" would be forced to close its doors and send students elsewhere for an education.

Dr. Maram Clifford has asked for information of the financial operations and practices of the district. The results do not look promising.

## Dilemma

Teneforth Public School District is facing certain state monitoring and likely closure if the new superintendent Dr. Maram Clifford cannot turn around the practices of fiscal responsibility in the district. She has taken a position in a district plagued by financial irresponsibility.

Reports indicate that many of her campuses are not compliant. Less than half of the campuses have met the Gold Standard requirements. Two have been designated "No Confidence" campuses. Dr. Maram Clifford has a short time to turn around the campuses and prepare them for their next round of ratings from the state.

## Questions

1. What's the biggest fiscal compliance issue Teneforth School District is facing? Why?
2. How would you resolve that issue?
3. What would closing the school district look like for parents? What is the impact of such an action?
4. What procedures should Dr. Maram Clifford put in place to ensure fiscal responsibility?

## CASE STUDY: EVERY CHILD MATTERS

Suburban district; Ethics and Professional Norms 2b, c

### Background

When Riley McMasters became the superintendent of Friedman Public Schools, she brought Carly Birch with her. The two women had worked together in a previous district, and they considered themselves student-centered leaders who knew how to produce student performance results. They were also best friends.

Friedman Public was going to need all the help it could get. In fact, that's why the school board unanimously voted for McMasters as their new superintendent. She had an impressive track record and an equally long runway. The board felt she would poise the district for exceptional success.

The Friedman Public Schools accountability director had just retired, and his position had been opened and advertised. Superintendent McMasters knew that Friedman Public needed to hire Carly Birch because Birch shared the same passion and drive for success. Who better to lead testing and accountability? The superintendent encouraged her friend to apply for the position.

"There's no guarantee, of course, for the job," said the superintendent. "You'll have to win everyone over." Then she winked at her friend.

Birch applied, was interviewed, and was recommended for the directorship. The board approved the recommendation, and Carly Birch was hired.

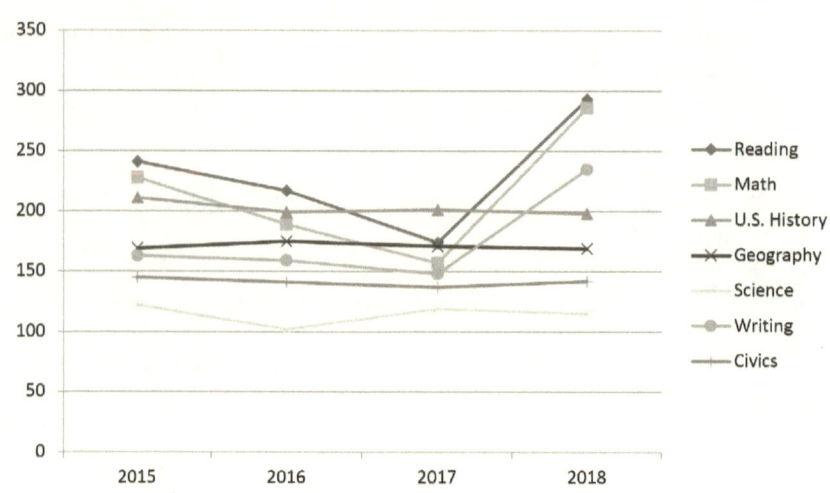

Figure 2.5. Friedman Public School District Longitudinal NAEP Scores

Table 2.6. Three Improvement Targets—Reading, Math, and Writing—and Other Subjects

| Year | Reading | Math | U.S. History | Geography | Science | Writing | Civics |
|---|---|---|---|---|---|---|---|
| 2015 | 241 | 228 | 211 | 169 | 122 | 163 | 145 |
| 2016 | 217 | 189 | 199 | 175 | 102 | 159 | 141 |
| 2017 | 174 | 157 | 201 | 171 | 119 | 148 | 137 |
| 2018 | 293 | 286 | 198 | 169 | 115 | 235 | 142 |

"Welcome to Friedman Public, my friend," said the superintendent.

McMasters and Birch settled in and got to work, collaborating with the campus leaders on projects throughout the year. Based on previous national assessment scores, the district identified three improvement targets: reading, math, and writing (see figure 2.5 and tables 2.6).

The district relied on data from curriculum-based assessments to monitor academic progress. The results were not encouraging. Approximately half the students were on track in reading, and only a third of them were on track in math. The teachers scored student compositions holistically, and they reported strong growth.

"Make no mistake, these scores must go up," said Superintendent McMasters. "We are all expecting great things this year, especially from you, Carly. I already told everyone on the board you would do it, no doubt about it."

## Issue

Carly Birch understood that her job was on the line. She had to prove that she could successfully lead this new group of educators. More importantly, she wanted the schools to see that their students could perform as well if not better than students anywhere in the nation.

Birch met with the principals in order to better understand how well the new initiatives were working. A few of the principals were hopeful, but most felt as though no one would see dramatic growth for a couple of years.

The accountability director felt as though change needed to happen a lot quicker. If need be, she would take matters into her own hands and *make* it happen.

Birch resolved that everyone would see improved student achievement. After collecting the tests and answer documents, she worked alone to verify and assemble the materials for shipment to the national student clearinghouse.

When the scores came back, Superintendent McMasters was ecstatic. She hugged Carly Birch and said, "I knew you could do it! I just had no idea these scores would be this awesome. The school board is thrilled. Congratulations!"

The superintendent went on to explain how the district would celebrate, and several education publications wanted to write articles about the turnaround in Friedman Public.

## Dilemma

Superintendent McMasters just hung up the phone in her office. All morning she had been talking to the State Education Agency and national assessment officials.

They told her that they had conclusive proof that the national assessment scores in Friedman Public this year were bogus. The test results were greatly skewed. McMasters asked how there could be such a big discrepancy in testing. After all, wasn't national assessment supposed to be highly respected? How could there be a question about test integrity?

"It's not the test," said the national assessment official. "A large number of answer documents were altered. Someone erased the original answers and re-bubbled them."

Only one person had unrestricted access to the documents.

Carly Birch.

## Questions

1. What do the scores in reading, math, and writing suggest? What about the U.S. history, science, and civics scores? What are the implications for any campus-based practices, like CBAs and holistic scoring?

2. How would you advise Superintendent McMasters to handle the concerns regarding test integrity? What can she tell parents?
3. Should Superintendent McMasters have hired her best friend?
4. How could a superintendent make sure that any test administration is done with integrity?
5. Are you in favor of paper tests or online tests? Explain your rationale.

## CASE STUDY: TOMATOE, TOMATO, WHAT'S YOUR IMAGO?

Suburban district; Ethics and Professional Norms 2d, e

### Background

The Ford Public Schools superintendent, Nidal Wayne, felt as though he had successfully launched another school year. In his three years in the district as its top academic officer, Superintendent Nidal Wayne saw steady increases in student performance in reading.

Unfortunately, he had also seen a steady decline in student performance in mathematics.

Superintendent Nidal Wayne began the academic year by meeting with his cabinet and the school administrators from around the district. Together, they determined that (1) performance in mathematics was indeed an issue and (2) more data were necessary to understand what the challenges were.

Superintendent Nidal Wayne provided campuses with the data they needed to drill down and analyze where students needed more support. Every campus had its own grade-level information, including passing percentages, performance on each objective, and data analysis of how subpopulations answered each of the questions. The human resources department provided the principals with information about how many years of experience each teacher has.

The campuses originally wanted to visit campuses in the districts that experienced similar scores to theirs, but Superintendent Nidal Wayne talked them into visiting the one district in the area that seemed to be doing well by its students: Dandelion Public School District.

Chris Johnson, the superintendent at Dandelion, had been cordial and welcoming. She met with the Ballentine principals, while their teachers visited classrooms to see math instruction in action. The Ballentine teachers were impressed by what they saw. The Dandelion teachers were using the latest research-based strategies in the classroom, and they also relied on a computer-based program that adaptively met kids' needs when it came to reinforcing math skills.

The Ballentine teachers were eager to do the same things back in their own district.

In the meantime, with the year under way, Superintendent Nidal Wayne will go to the annual Fall Area Superintendents' Meeting. The purpose of the meeting is for superintendents to gather together without interruption so that they can figure out what's working or not working in their districts. Hopefully, they can share ideas.

The following chart (see table 2.7) is what the superintendents will discuss as a group at their Fall Area Superintendents' Meeting.

## Issue

The area superintendents greeted each other and sat down to discuss the overall performance at each of their districts.

Superintendent Johnson, of Dandelion Public schools, looked directly at Billy Jenner, the superintendent at Exeter Public Schools.

"So how are things, Billy?" she asked.

Everyone knew the answer to that question. They had seen the scores at Exeter.

"How are things?" asked Superintendent Jenner, "They're awful, that's how they are. We keep getting some of the worst scores each year. And I can tell you why, too. We have some of *those* kids—you know the ones I mean—that keep bringing down our scores. They come to school because their parents want free babysitting, free food, and free school. It's clear these kids don't care. They don't even take an interest in what's going on. And it's not like our teachers don't know what they're doing. They are some of the most experienced teachers ever. That's why I told them at the beginning of the year that if the scores don't improve, heads are gonna roll. I mean it, too."

Stunned into silence, the superintendents said nothing, while the Exeter superintendent harangued every subpopulation and ethnicity he perceived had brought down the scores at Exeter. He was so loud that the leaders from other tables in the room kept looking over at the table making all the commotion.

The Applewhite and Churchton superintendents agreed that it was a shame the way education was changing.

## Dilemma

At the annual Fall Area Superintendents' Meeting, one superintendent has spoken negatively about his students. He complained that they are too diverse, coming from different ethnicities and representing many different subpopulations. The demographics in his district have changed, but the instruction has

**Table 2.7. Assessment Scores**

| Assessment Scores | Applewhite | Ford | Churchton | Dandelion | Exeter |
|---|---|---|---|---|---|
| **Reading (R)** | 79 | 83 | 88 | 86 | 74 |
| **Math (M)** | 75 | 67 | 65 | 81 | 59 |
| **Enrollment** | 11,321 | 14,456 | 8,793 | 16,547 | 19,654 |
| **Gender** | | | | | |
| Female—R | 84 | 89 | 82 | 85 | 80 |
| Female—M | 72 | 79 | 64 | 82 | 62 |
| Male—R | 72 | 62 | 74 | 83 | 48 |
| Male—M | 78 | 54 | 67 | 85 | 54 |
| Gender Neutral—R | — | 58 | — | — | 73 |
| Gender Neutral—M | — | 52 | — | — | 36 |
| **Race/Ethnicity** | | | | | |
| African American—R | 78 | 81 | 78 | 80 | 65 |
| African American—M | 76 | 60 | 62 | 75 | 57 |
| Hispanic—R | 67 | 82 | 82 | 77 | 68 |
| Hispanic—M | 72 | 61 | 78 | 76 | 56 |
| White—R | 83 | 84 | 90 | 89 | 82 |
| White—M | 84 | 65 | 75 | 87 | 80 |
| Native American—R | — | — | — | 78 | — |
| Native American—M | — | — | — | 73 | — |
| Pacific Islander/Asian—R | 86 | — | — | — | — |
| Pacific Islander/Asian—M | 90 | — | — | — | — |
| **Special Populations** | | | | | |
| Gifted—R | 86 | 92 | 93 | 95 | 90 |
| Gifted—M | 84 | 87 | 83 | 91 | 87 |
| Special education—R | 64 | 68 | 79 | 75 | 66 |
| Special education—M | 59 | 65 | 60 | 73 | 51 |
| Bilingual/ELL—R | 55 | 84 | 80 | 77 | 65 |
| Bilingual/ELL—M | 67 | 64 | 76 | 76 | 55 |
| Migrant—R | 68 | 85 | 84 | 71 | — |
| Migrant—M | 70 | 63 | 77 | 72 | — |
| At-Risk—R | 58 | 79 | 76 | 72 | 65 |
| At-Risk—M | 72 | 69 | 69 | 66 | 55 |
| Homeless—R | — | 65 | — | 56 | — |
| Homeless—M | — | 61 | — | 48 | — |
| **% of Teachers** | Applewhite | Ford | Churchton | Dandelion | Exeter |
| 0–1 Yrs. Experience | 10 | 30 | 15 | 20 | 0 |
| 2–5 Yrs. Experience | 15 | 20 | 20 | 10 | 5 |
| 5–10 Yrs. Experience | 25 | 25 | 35 | 20 | 5 |
| 11–15 Yrs. Experience | 30 | 10 | 20 | 25 | 10 |
| 16–20 Yrs. Experience | 10 | 10 | 5 | 20 | 15 |
| 20+ Yrs. Experience | 10 | 5 | 5 | 5 | 65 |

not. Although his teachers have many years of experience, he told them that if they did not improve student performance, they, in essence, would be fired.

As Superintendent Jenner complained and stereotyped student groups, he became louder and louder. His rant interrupted other conversations.

"Stop it!" said Superintendent Johnson. "You're making a spectacle of yourself, and it's clear you have a problem!"

"The problem is your *imago*," said Superintendent Nidal Wayne. "You have this mental image of the perfect student. Your *imago* is this unconscious perception that this perfect kid is out there somewhere, eager to come to your district to learn. The kid is going to hang on every word your teachers say, and he or she will learn easily. Other kids like this one will learn no matter what. But that's not the business we're in. Times have changed."

## Questions

1. What do the scores at Exeter Public Schools reveal?
2. Should the district leaders have allowed Superintendent Jenner to rant? Why or why not?
3. Superintendent Nidal Wayne said, "That's not the business we're in." How would you describe the business of a superintendent?
4. What would you do if you were Chris Johnson? What if you were one of the superintendents at another table?
5. What follow-up could the superintendents take?

*Chapter 3*

# Creating a Sense of Belonging, Inclusivity in a Post-Pandemic World

This chapter is about the values of diversity, equity, inclusion, and belongingness that are embedded into our school district's mission and further emphasized in the goals developed by the school district and school superintendent's office.

Let's start at the very beginning. Creating a sense of belonging for students means that the school superintendent needs some help. Start by creating a taskforce or a working group to make recommendations on how to best support students of color and historically underserved communities in the school district. And a superintendent's community advisory group is a good idea as well. This can include:

1. Addressing opportunity gaps facing specific student groups
2. Bringing deeper cultural context and awareness to classroom instruction
3. Genuinely engaging families from historically underrepresented communities in the district
4. Taking steps to enhance and support diverse staff
5. Improve school climate by providing tools and protocols to address inequitable behavior.

By aligning with the district mission, vision, and goals, schools desire to achieve the district equity goal to create a community where all members feel valued. In recognition of our diverse school community, school districts will ensure for all an equitable education experience in which race, ethnicity, class, gender identity, sexuality, and disability are not predictors of student success. Let's see how school superintendents have grappled with issues of diversity, equity, inclusivity, and belongingness.

## CASE STUDY: LOW INCOME, HIGH EXPECTATIONS

Suburban District; Equity and Cultural Responsiveness 3c; Meaningful Engagement of Families and Community 8b; School Improvement 10a

### Background

Dr. Muhammad Wooden has just completed his second year as the superintendent of Ft. Bainbridge Public Schools.

When the academic accountability results were released in the summer, every campus in the district had improved its scores in math, reading, and science, except one: Tinkerton High School (THS). One of six high schools in the district, Tinkerton was the oldest in the community. THS first opened its doors in 1951 as the district's flagship campus, and its enrollment has steadily grown from several hundred students to nearly 2,400 ninth through 12th graders. Although the campus has a high student enrollment, the school serves one of the most impoverished communities in the district.

The houses surrounding the campus are nearly as old as the campus itself. Many of the homes are in disrepair, and vandalism is a serious concern in several of the neighborhoods around Tinkerton.

Most notably, the students taking the ELA, math, and science state assessments failed to demonstrate greater year-to-year growth on the exams than the other five high schools in the district (see table 3.1). Student assessment results indicated that the high schoolers were losing ground rather than gaining it. There was little evidence of retention from year to year, especially as students progressed from 9th to 12th grades.

In addition, 93.8 percent of the four-year cohort students in the 9th grade were identified as being "on track" for graduation. In the five-year cohort, 84.6 percent of the students were on track for graduating, and 79.2 percent were on track in the six-year cohort. Not surprisingly, less than 25 percent of the students at Tinkerton High School were considered college and career ready.

Table 3.1. Academic Achievement

|  | *State Metric Value* | *LEA Metric Value* | *Possible Points* | *Points Earned* |
|---|---|---|---|---|
| Proficiency in ELA | 56.63% | 45.64% | 56.25 | 25.67 |
| Proficiency in Math | 45.13% | 38.86% | 56.25 | 21.86 |
| Proficiency in Science | 47.45% | 36.19% | 25.00 | 9.05 |

Parent meetings during the past two years had been poorly attended. The school held numerous meetings during the first couple of grading periods, but after that, the number of meetings declined. During the spring semester, there was usually one or two meetings about graduation. Again, parent turnout was low.

To Dr. Muhammad Wooden, it seemed that the Tinkerton students were losing academic ground, and some of the district stakeholders accepted the results as inevitable.

"It's an old school. Really old," said one of the board members. "Tinkerton's seen better days. You can't expect much else."

"We all saw this coming," said another. "The best thing to do is close the school and send the kids to the other high schools."

The director of student services pointed out that "even getting the kids to school on a regular basis is tough. There's no draw, no attraction to make them want to go to school."

## Issue

The superintendent, Dr. Muhammad Wooden, has seen a surge of academic growth during his two-year stint in the Ft. Bainbridge Public School District. Five out of the six high schools are performing well. They have met or exceeded state expectations, and students are on track for graduation as well as meeting college and career readiness requirements.

One school, Tinkerton High School, has lost academic ground. Students showed poor academic performance on recent state assessments, and the scores indicated that there is no growth, only regression. Students are not graduating on time, and they are ill-prepared for college and career readiness.

Some of the school board members and even the district employees seem to have given up on reviving Tinkerton High School and energizing the students and their parents.

## Dilemma

Tinkerton High School is one of six high schools in the Ft. Bainbridge Public School District. It has the lowest accountability scores in the district. Members of the school board and some of the central office employees do not seem surprised by the assessment results. They insist that they saw it coming, citing the old building and disengaged community as reasons for the failure.

THS, however, has an enrollment of 2,400 students, and dividing the student population up to attend the other district high schools would make their enrollments swell by nearly 500 students. In addition, the poor performance has an impact on the overall accountability results of the Ft. Bainbridge Public School District.

Tinkerton High School is in need of immediate and extensive intervention. The assessment scores for students at THS indicate that the school is not reaching students and preparing them for college and career readiness.

## Questions

1. What other data do you recommend that Dr. Muhammad Wooden consider in his evaluation of Tinkerton High School's needs?
2. Is it better to save the old school or send the THS students elsewhere? Justify your answer.
3. What can Dr. Muhammad Wooden do to change the mindset of the school board members about the decline of Tinkerton High School?
4. Should the superintendent launch a revitalization project for Tinkerton High School? Why or why not?
5. If you were the superintendent in Ft. Bainbridge Public Schools, what are the first action steps you would take?

## CASE STUDY: PREPARING FOR DIVERSITY

Rural district; Equity and Cultural Responsiveness 3a, b, c

### Background

Arthur Dumas is the superintendent at Greenmoor Public School District. He has held this position for twelve years. The district encompasses several hundred miles of rural land, and the schools are the main focus in this community. The campuses disseminate information to parents and neighborhoods, and they provide additional student services, such as low-cost vaccinations and year-round library services for students.

"We'd do so much more," lamented Dr. Dumas, "But there's more need than money. Our student demographics are changing, too. I don't know how we'll get everyone the education they deserve."

Dr. Dumas meant his remarks as positive—an attempt to show that he truly cared for the changing population in the community and wanted to meet the needs of the families and their children.

His passion in education focused on two things: advocating for the state and federal funding his children in the district earned and making sure their resources were used wisely. The problem, as he saw it, was that change had arrived, and not everyone had been ready for it. Just a decade ago, the district was 80 percent White, 10 percent Black, and 10 percent Hispanic.

Dr. Dumas tried to tell the community that nothing stayed the same forever, not even Greenmoor Public School District and the population it served. As the years had gone by, the population became more diversified. So did the needs of the students. The data that the superintendent and the principals were looking at revealed some interesting truths (see tables 3.2 and 3.3).

The attitude of some of the school leaders, however, didn't change.

"Look here," said the high school principal Frank Le Torneau. "We've done a pretty good job educating kids in these parts. That says we know what we're doing. Anyone new to the district will have to adapt to our program."

Several other principals murmured their agreement.

The high school principal continued. "I'd venture to say we do an outstanding job at our schools, and we save the taxpayers plenty of money. Our leftover money at the end of the year gets sent back to Central so they can start the next school year or send it back to the state."

Dr. Dumas squinted his eyes and lowered his reading glasses to look at the principals. Did he just hear what he thought he heard?

## Issue

Superintendent Dr. Arthur Dumas had seen his rural district change and grow and change in the twelve years he had overseen the education of the children in his rural community. During this time, he had seen the student demographics change from predominantly White to more diversified ethnicities. Recently, the White population was no longer the largest sub-group. There were more Hispanics than any other group in the Greenmoor community.

During his tenure as superintendent, Dr. Dumas had advocated for being prepared for the change that they would one day face.

That change had arrived, but some of his school leaders, especially the high school principal, were adamant that the new students and their families conform to the old way of doing district business. Greenmoor Public Schools had always done a fine job in the past of meeting student needs. The leaders saw no reason to change.

They were proud of the job they were doing.

## Dilemma

Superintendent Dr. Dumas faced a three-fold challenge. His student demographics had been changing with each passing year, and so had the funding sources the district received. Culturally diverse students deserved an

**Table 3.2. Percentage of Students by Race and Ethnicity**

| Data Elements 2017–2018 | District/State | Value | 0%----------50%----------100% |
|---|---|---|---|
| Percentage of American Indian and Alaskan Native Students | District | 0.02% | |
| | State | 0% | |
| Percentage of Black Students | District | 21.2% | |
| | State | 10.1% | |
| Percentage of Hispanic Students | District | 48.0% | |
| | State | 30.1% | |
| Percentage of Native Hawaiian or Other Pacific Islander Students | District | 0.01% | |
| | State | 0.01% | |
| Percentage of White Students | District | 29.5% | |
| | State | 59.7% | |

Table 3.3. Total Program Funding

| Data Elements 2021–2022 | District/State | Amount |
|---|---|---|
| Title I/School Readiness | District | $325,000 |
| | State | $8,725,000 |
| State Assessment and Accountability | District | $60,000 |
| | State | $360,000 |
| College and Career Awareness | District | $410,000 |
| | State | $490,000 |
| ELL Education and Bilingual Education | District | $50,000 |
| | State | $700,000 |
| Migrant Services and Education | District | $49,000 |
| | State | $400,500 |
| Homeless and At-Risk Youth | District | $12,000 |
| | State | $202,000 |
| Special Education | District | $3,900,000 |
| | State | $111,750,000 |
| School Turnaround | District | $200,250 |
| | State | $900,000 |
| Teacher Training | District | $4,000,000 |
| | | $55,000,000 |

education that could meet their specific needs, and every dollar was critical for providing that kind of education.

Today was the first time that Dr. Dumas heard the principals brag about continuing their old practices. Many of the leaders seemed unwilling to make accommodations for diversity, and they even sent back unused money for those children.

The schools were not meeting the needs of the changing population. They weren't even keeping up.

## Questions

1. What other data would you like to see presented?
2. Why might Dr. Dumas not have noticed these challenges before?
3. What's the best way to make sure that the students at Greenmoor Public School District receive the services to which they are entitled?
4. What training do the school leaders need? What about the teachers?
5. If you were Dr. Dumas, what are your next steps?

## CASE STUDY: HOW WE'VE ALWAYS DONE IT

Rural district; Mission, Vision, and Core Values 1c; Equity and Cultural Responsiveness 3a, b

## Background

Dwainville Independent School District (ISD) used to be a tiny community inconveniently located in the middle of nowhere. The rural district was the biggest employer in the area, and not only did everyone know everyone else, but they called each other by their first names, regardless of job title.

Most of the residents grew up together, and families helped each other out. They spent leisure time together, too, fishing in the nearby river or hunting in the fall. They had cookouts, high school football, and good memories of growing up in Dwainville.

As some of the older family matriarchs and patriarchs passed on, however, Dwainville began to change. It was gradual at first, but then the changes became more pronounced. The town added a grocery store, a couple of fast-food restaurants, several stop lights, and there was talk of a Walmart coming in, too.

Many of the adult children in these families, however, had sought jobs in urban areas. The population growth in Dwainville was the result of city people wanting to adopt what they thought would be a more idyllic lifestyle. The large parcels of land were subdivided, and neighborhoods took root where once crops stood in the fields and cattle grazed in pastures. The biggest neighborhood already had over 5,000 homes in it. More were being planned and built.

These new families brought more than just their children with them. They also brought diversity, and that was something Dwainville had little experience with.

Already the district was shocked by the realization that the subpopulation's performance on standardized assessments could come back to bite them (see table 3.4).

In the past, Dwainville ISD had no subpopulations to speak of. At least 99 percent of the students were White. Less than 1 percent of the students were identified for special education services. There were two bilingual children in the elementary school, but the school decided to immerse them in English since they weren't required to provide bilingual education services.

Table 3.4. Progress Results for Dwainville Independent School District

| Indicator: Achievement on State Assessment Performance and CCR Readiness | Percent Passing |
|---|---|
| Overall Student Performance | 81% |
| Economically Disadvantaged Student Performance | 26% |
| English Language Learner Student Performance | 37% |
| Special Education Student Performance | 19% |

Dwainville, with a current enrollment of approximately 3,000 students, always maintained that their students were far more than scoring on achievement tests. Their kids were multifaceted individuals with plenty of interests and options.

The district offered a robust extracurricular program for students, and in the past, it was well attended. The activities consisted of two categories: sports and Future Farmers of America, and most kids participated in something. Some of the kids participated in several activities (see table 3.5).

Some of the other issues about diversity weren't measurable on student achievement tests, but the differences were apparent, nonetheless. Dwainville ISD was once a Christian community, where faith in God and community prayer were important. Now, approximately 5 percent of the community was atheistic or agnostic. Another 15 percent associated themselves with religions other than Christianity.

Superintendent Ricky Meyers had to admit it. Dwainville had changed.

He hoped it was for the better.

## Issue

There had been rumblings, of which there were many, over the past eighteen months that the new parents were unhappy with the school district and with the administration. The parents felt as though their children's needs weren't being met.

At the beginning of this school year, they had asked for a variety of new extracurricular activities. Their children wanted to play soccer and start a

Table 3.5. Participating Students

| | Number of Students Participating | | |
|---|---|---|---|
| Activity | Elementary School | Middle School | High School |
| Football | 0 | 37 | 78 |
| Baseball | 0 | 21 | 32 |
| Basketball | 0 | 16 | 20 |
| Cheerleading | 14 | 15 | 40 |
| Band | 0 | 26 | 113 |
| Volleyball | 0 | 12 | 11 |
| Softball | 0 | 14 | 23 |
| FFA | 11 | 8 | 55 |
| Rodeo Club | 2 | 21 | 39 |
| Outdoor Adventurers Club | 0 | 0 | 17 |
| Fellowship of Christian Athletes | 0 | 0 | 6 |

technology club. They wanted to create a Go Green Initiative and a drama group, and they wanted to express themselves and their interests in the activities.

The administration turned down every request, insisting that Dwainville ISD offered plenty of diverse activities already. The students could choose from one of those, they said.

Clearly, the administration hadn't been listening. They continued doing business how they had always done it.

## Dilemma

Now a group of parents are demanding to see Superintendent Ricky Meyers. They are frustrated that their children cannot be involved in activities that interest them.

"Not everyone likes football, and not everyone is a cowboy," said one of the parents. Those gathered around her murmured their agreement. "Our children have a right to have their cultural interests and needs met."

"Ma'am, we're doing the best we can. This is what we offer. Take it or leave it," said the superintendent.

A single figure dressed in a suit and tie emerged from the throng and said, "No, I don't think that's how it's going to work out at all." The man handed Ricky Meyers his business card. "You see," said the man, "I want to talk with you about how you're denying the children of these taxpayers their rights. We also need to talk about that prayer thing in your school meetings. The American Federation of Labor and Congress of Industrial Organizations (AFL-CIO) believes you've violated our Resolution 44."

## Questions

1. Why doesn't the Dwainville Elementary School have to provide bilingual education to the two students they have? Should they offer bilingual education anyway?
2. The statement assessment scores reveal a large gap between what could be called Dwainville's former population and the students currently enrolled in the DISD schools. What is the cause of the disparity?
3. The second data set is for student participation in extracurricular activities. What do the enrollment numbers show?
4. How would you advise the superintendent to handle his inevitable conversation with the AFL-CIO representative?
5. How could this scenario have been avoided?

## CASE STUDY: EMOTIONAL AND BEHAVIORAL DISORDERS (EBD) IN PINE TREE

Rural district; Equity and Cultural Responsiveness 3a, d; Community of Care and Support for Students 5e; School Improvement 10f

### Background

The rural Pine Tree school district is experiencing new growth and new behaviors. Once a small community, the Pine Tree area has witnessed considerable growth because families are moving out of the cities and into the country. Pine Tree is also near a military base, and many of the military personnel's children attend school in the district. Many of the families and especially their children have experienced trauma in one form or another.

Not surprisingly, there has been an increase in off-task and disruptive behavior in the Pine Tree classrooms. Superintendent Garland Shepherd has heard the campus administrators complain that their time is taken up by impulsive, disruptive, and aggressive behaviors.

The National Science Teaching Association has identified how teachers refer to the behaviors they see in the classroom. Teachers have observed the following student behaviors:

1. initiating aggressive behavior and reacting aggressively toward others.
2. displaying bullying, threatening, or intimidating behavior.
3. physically abusing others.
4. deliberately destructing others' property.
5. showing little empathy and concern for the feelings, wishes, and well-being of others.
6. showing callous behavior toward others and lack of feelings of guilt or remorse.
7. readily informing on their companions and blaming others for their own misdeeds
8. disrupting classroom activities
9. being impulsive
10. being inattentive and distractible
11. being preoccupied
12. not following or appearing to care about classroom rules
13. having poor concentration
14. showing resistance to change and transitions in routines

15. often speaking out with irrelevant information or without regard to turn-taking rules
16. demonstrating aggressive behavior
17. being regularly absent from school
18. consistently blaming others for their dishonesty
19. having low self-esteem
20. having difficulty working in groups
21. demonstrating self-injurious behavior
22. not being able to apply social rules related to others' personal space and belongings
23. often being manipulative of situations

In response, the teachers want to implement helpful strategies for students who exhibit behavioral disorders. They estimate that 30 percent of their instructional time is spent redirecting off-task behavior. By helping students with emotional and behavioral disorders stay on task, the rest of the class can also remain on task. The teachers have requested further professional development on ways to intervene and redirect. They want to learn about trauma-informed care in the classroom.

## Issue

In Pine Tree, behavioral discipline data are rarely collected and analyzed over time. The Pine Tree educators agree that data help them make informed decisions; they have plenty of academic data. However, many times, the teachers are asked to fill out lengthy behavior forms by hand. These data collection sheets become part of a student's file and part of a larger collection system, but the forms create data silos. All of the data are reviewed independently, rather than as a correlation.

To make matters worse, most behavior data collected each academic year are discarded, and students begin anew with a fresh slate.

Starting fresh each year allows students to learn from their mistakes and make better choices about their actions and reactions. Unfortunately, the system does not allow teachers and campus administrators to do the same thing. They have no system to collect, mask, and analyze the data. They, too, start fresh each year, but they are unprepared to deal with emotional and behavioral disorders and provide trauma-informed care.

## Dilemma

Superintendent Garland Shepherd recognizes the need for intervention in the classroom. The Pine Tree area is growing in population, and the military base expects to be open for many years to come. Shepherd's studies infer that as much as 2–6 percent of all students have emotional and behavioral disorders (EBD). In his district of 10,000 students, that means 200–600 students have emotional and behavioral disorders. The special education department reports that less than 1 percent of their students have been identified as having EBD.

Mr. Shepherd is considering hiring additional staff to assist with the expected increase in identified EBD behaviors. He also wants teachers to have the skills they need to intervene with trauma-informed care strategies. However, he has no data to take to the school board to prove that the need exists.

## Questions

1. What can the Pine Tree district do to collect student discipline data and analyze it for patterns and trends?
2. Who should be involved in the data collection effort?
3. Should Shepherd create positions and hire EBD staff? Why or why not?
4. How would these positions be paid for?
5. If so, how many positions would you recommend? What would their job description be?
6. If not, what alternative initiatives should be considered?
7. How should the community be involved in these decisions?

## CASE STUDY: PERIOD SHAMING

Suburban district; Equity and Cultural Responsiveness 3a, d; Community of Care and Support for Students 5e

### Background

Bryant Middle School had had a bullying problem for some time. The principal, Rose de Leon, served in her third year at the Title I school. Attendance (82%) and academics (math 44%, reading 58%) were suffering—schoolwide scores had plummeted since Mrs. De Leon took the helm.

Last year, the campus administration handled 1,517 discipline referrals for the student body of 700 students. When the campus analyzed the disciplinary data, 65 percent of the referrals were related to bullying.

"And these are only the reported incidents," noted one of the counselors.

This year, the administration already reviewed more than 2,200 incidents. Again, most of the referrals had something to do with bullying.

## Issue

Lately, menstruating girls have become the target of bullies. Many of the boys began picking on girls having their periods, bullying them about a physiological process over which they had no control. Sometimes the boys snickered at the girls who needed to step out of the classroom. Other times they made remarks about the girls' periods.

"What's the matter? Is the Red River flowing again?" they'd ask in class.

Even some girls had taken up bullying some of their poorest female peers. The girls didn't do their bullying in class. They took care of business in the restrooms, where they singled out girls who didn't have feminine hygiene products like pads. The girls who were being bullied came from low-income families, and they didn't have the means to purchase the feminine hygiene products they needed.

"What'cha doing in there—using leaves again? Or are you gonna wring that thing out and use it again?" Then the laughter would follow.

As a result, menstruating girls chose to stay home during their cycle, which could be anywhere from three to nine days at a time.

The counselors suggested to Principal De Leon that the school provide a menstruation station for all girls to use. The school could provide the hygiene products for free to *all* girls who needed them.

"What do you think we are, a Walmart?" snapped Mrs. De Leon. "The school budget can barely cover costs now. How would we even afford something like that? And what's next? Do I have to start buying everyone toothpaste and a toothbrush, too?"

## Dilemma

It wasn't long before the parents learned why the girls were being bullied, and they brought it up in a Town Hall meeting between the principal, the Superintendent Dwayne Disdale and his cabinet, and the community. The stakeholders had come together to discuss ways to improve attendance and increase academic scores.

The topic of discussion changed quickly.

As one parent put it, "Our daughters are staying away from school because they're not getting support from you people. You're not stepping in, and the bullies are stepping up. What does it take, a suicide for you to provide the basic needs for them?"

A group of like-minded parents quickly rallied around the parent.

Another parent jumped to the microphone, jabbing his finger into the air. "That's *your* job as a parent, you low-life. You need to take care of your own kids, just like everybody else."

Murmurs of agreement and nodding heads erupted after this statement.

The parents argued back and forth for a while, some at the mics and some in their seats. Within moments, a brawl broke out. Parents were so polarized over the issue that they took swings at each other.

## Questions

1. What should Superintendent Disdale do first?
2. Is menstrual bullying really an issue? Why or why not?
3. If you were the superintendent, what's your response to Mrs. De Leon?
4. How could menstruation stations solve many of the school's challenges with attendance, discipline, and academics?
5. With no money in the budget set aside for student hygiene, how could schools fund menstruation stations?
6. Would you encourage menstruation stations in your district? Why or why not?

*Chapter 4*

# Creating Communities to Champion All Students

The context of leadership in the public school has become increasingly complex with the pressures of high-stakes testing and accountability, changing student demographics, and financial challenges. Stakeholders must work together to develop effective strategies to increase student academic performance. Successful superintendents must optimize learning by fostering relationships across the district to validate the contributions of all constituents. This demands that leaders change from the traditional bureaucracy to a model of collaboration, redefining organizations as communities. To do this, they must listen, create spaces for dialogue, and encourage risk-taking. The literature on community seeks to provide models for schools to adopt in an effort to build relationships that significantly impact teaching and learning. Those relationships occur internally within a school and school district as well as externally with the wider community.

Shields and Edwards (2005) suggest that the fundamental problem faced by educational leaders is that they do not practice effective dialogue—dialogue that involves understanding, empathy, relationship, and "listening with the ears and with the heart." Good educational leaders are aware of their relationships with those that surround them and practice real dialogue with students, colleagues, parents, and administrators. The authors believe that dialogue empowers educational communities to focus on healthy relationships and deeper understanding and to be more inclusive and democratic. School superintendents must ensure that all members in the community learn to speak together with moral voices, where each perspective is valued and no one truth is universal (Shields and Edwards 2005).

This chapter focuses on the critical need for acknowledging and, moreover, building a community of difference where diversity is valued and voices are heard. The motivation for the book and this chapter is to develop an understanding of the complexity of the duty of a superintendent, who is tasked to lead a district, as he or she attempts to develop a strong sense of district community.

## CASE STUDY: NAVIGATING CHARTERED WATERS

Urban district; Community of Care and Support for Students 5c; Operations and Management 9d

### Background

Dr. Layann Hackner has begun her first year as the superintendent of the Gwenforth School District, located in an urban area that has seen considerable growth in the past three years. Families are eager to find housing in the district because Gwenforth has developed a reputation for meeting the diverse needs of all of its students.

One of the ways the district has been able to serve its student population is by opening charter schools uniquely designed to provide an education to students who may be underserved by traditional schools and systems of instruction. Many of the students enrolled in the charter schools are interested in careers, but not a traditional path to them that includes college.

The district has three charter schools within its boundaries: Integrity Charter, Olympus Charter, and Unicorn Charter. Each charter campus was designed to meet a particular student need, as follows:

- Integrity Charter: Open enrollment charter that teaches applied science and mathematics. Graduating students earn professional certificates.
- Olympus Charter: Open-enrollment charter that teaches computer science, networking, and infrastructure design. Many graduates work in technology fields.
- Unicorn Charter: Open-enrollment charter that teaches visual and performing arts, as well as creative writing. Graduating students become artists, and 40 percent set up their own shops and studios to sell their art.

Each high school in Gwenforth also has its own unique demographics:

- Lincoln High School: Public high school with demographics of 30 percent White, 35 percent Hispanic, and 30 percent African American. Low special education population, high GT population. Students consistently demonstrate high performance on state assessment, and 79 percent go on to college.

Table 4.1. Per Pupil Expenditures by Campus at Gwenforth School District

| | Per Pupil Expenditures | Student Enrollment | Met State Accountability | Met Federal Accountability |
|---|---|---|---|---|
| Integrity Charter | $11,953 | 499 | N | N |
| Olympus Charter | $11,695 | 568 | Y | N |
| Unicorn Charter | $9,827 | 337 | N | N |
| Lincoln High School | $15,575 | 2100 | Y | Y |
| Jefferson High School | $16,110 | 2300 | Y | N |
| Smith High School | 14,754 | 1900 | Y | Y |

- Jefferson High School: Public high school with demographics of 20 percent White, 65 percent Hispanic, and 15 percent African American. This campus scores low on accountability reports and has a 55 percent ELL population. Jefferson also receives the largest amount of Title II funds for bilingual/ELL education. In every graduating class, 78 percent of the students are accepted into college.
- Smith High School: Public high school with evenly distributed demographics across races, but has a high special education population (15.6%). The seniors have a 67 percent college acceptance rate.

One of the concerns expressed by the school board when they hired the superintendent Dr. Layann Hackner included inequity in funding. The per pupil expenditures at each campus varied greatly (see table 4.1).

Superintendent Layann Hackner was surprised by the data that showed how much money the district spent on the students in traditional campuses compared to spending at the charter campuses.

## Issue

The superintendent, Dr. Layann Hackner, accepted the top leadership position in Gwenforth School District, and one of her first tasks is to review the disparity and inequities in funding at each of the high schools. Per pupil expenditures vary by as much as $8,000 across high school campuses in the same district.

The students at each of the high schools have unique interests. Not all students are interested in pursuing a college education, but some have made college and career readiness a priority.

Not only are the funding levels greatly varied at each high school. The charter campuses have a demonstrated difficulty in meeting not only the state but also federal accountability requirements.

## Dilemma

Superintendent must formulate a per pupil expenditure plan that is equitable, and she must be able to back it up with a rationale that makes sense to the school board and the community.

Each of the high schools has unique missions and goals. The charter schools especially have unique focuses, and the traditional campuses attend to the needs of special student subpopulations.

In addition, the prior expenditure practices have not been proven to be effective, as measured by accountability scores for state and federal requirements.

## Questions

1. What could explain the disparity in per pupil funding allotments across the six high schools?
2. What's the most equitable way to distribute the per pupil funding allotments among all six high schools in the district?
3. What other data do you recommend that the superintendent, Dr. Layann Hackner, review before making her decision?
4. If you were the superintendent of Gwenforth Public Schools, how would you explain your decisions to the community and the school board?

## CASE STUDY: GETTING THEM ALL ACROSS THE STAGE

Urban district; Curriculum, Instruction, and Assessment 4a; Community of Care and Support for Students 5e

## Background

Interim superintendent Isaac Foster has been an academic leader in the Creek City Public School District for two decades.

He began his education career as a history teacher, helped with some coaching during sports seasons, and eventually transitioned into educational administrator. He worked his way from assistant principal to high school principal, and then two years later took on a role as the assistant superintendent for curriculum and instruction in the same district, where he remained until recently.

Foster was aware of the low graduation rates at Creek City H.S. They were low when he was the principal there, and they continued to plummet when he transitioned to central office administration. Other matters had occupied

Table 4.2. Graduation Rates by Campus, District, City, and State

| Cohort Year | High School Graduation Rates | | | |
| --- | --- | --- | --- | --- |
|  | Creek City | District | City | State |
| Four-Year Cohort | 58 | 77 | 82 | 87 |
| Five-Year Cohort | 45 | 79 | 85 | 86 |
| Six-Year Cohort | 54 | 73 | 78 | 84 |

the former superintendent, including severe budget cuts to state and federally funded programs. The other high schools had sufficiently high graduation rates to keep the district off the radar and out of trouble, and Creek City High School seemed to have been neglected (see table 4.2).

Improving graduation rates at Creek City High School had not been an issue until now.

New requirements from the state education agency focused everyone's attention on the graduation rates at Creek City. If the school did not show a marked improvement in each year's cohort group among all subpopulations, the campus and the district would lose its satisfactory accountability rating, and possibly its accreditation status if the problem was not resolved within a two-year period.

The former superintendent resigned a mere two weeks ago, and the school board named Isaac Foster as the Interim Superintendent until a permanent district leader could be found.

## Issue

Interim Superintendent Isaac Foster understands the issues centering on the low graduation rates at Creek City High School better than anyone else.

During his time employed as the district's assistant superintendent for C&I, Mr. Foster saw the annual results for the high school. He dutifully had meetings with the campus principal to discuss raising the rates. The principal insisted at the beginning of every new school year that his team was working on the issue. Mr. Foster allowed the principal to make the changes, and when the results were released, the principal was just as shocked as Mr. Foster that the only change that had taken place was a drop in the scores.

Now the issue faced Mr. Foster head-on.

The national search firm hired to locate candidates for the position of superintendent warned the school board, and Mr. Foster, that the search could take six months or longer. The board was in no hurry; they assured the firm. They wanted to find the right candidate, even if that candidate had been right there with them all along.

If Mr. Foster were the right candidate, he would have to resolve the issue of the dropping graduation rates.

## Dilemma

Interim Superintendent Isaac Foster must determine the reason for the low graduation rates at Creek City High School. Graduation rates at this campus have been historically low for years.

During this time, Mr. Foster has been the assistant superintendent for curriculum and instruction. Before taking on this leadership role, Mr. Foster was the principal at Creek City High School for two years. The graduation rates then were also the lowest in the district.

Mr. Foster must address and correct the issue; if he does not or cannot, his educational career may be finished.

## Questions

1. How do Creek City High School's cohort graduation rates stack up against other graduation rates in the district, the city, and the state? How would you go about identifying the issue at Creek City High School regarding its low graduation rates?
2. Identify the stakeholders who need to resolve the issue of the low graduation rates at Creek City High School. Why should these groups be involved in the graduation initiative?
3. What's the most equitable way to distribute the per pupil funding allotments among all six high schools in the district?
4. If you were the incoming superintendent, would you keep Mr. Foster in the position of assistant superintendent for curriculum and instruction? Why or why not? What about the principal of Creek City High School?
5. If you were the interim superintendent in this situation, would you ask to be considered as a superintendent candidate of this district? Why or why not?

## CASE STUDY: TO V OR NOT TO V

Urban district; Curriculum, Instruction, and Assessment 4d, e

## Background

As the interim superintendent, Dr. Fatimah Williams oversees the Metro School District, an urban district that educates approximately 20,000 students, many of whom are low-income and have recently immigrated. The students in this district come from various cultural backgrounds, but they all seem to have one thing in common: their parents want their children to learn as much as possible.

A study in the *International Journal of Education and Practice* points out that "meta-analyses suggest that online courses are about as effective as face-to-face courses. Blended learning courses, however, tend to be the best of all, with the important caveat that students also tend to perform more work in blended learning courses."

In 2020, however, due to COVID-19 when the district had to change its instructional approach in a week's time from traditional in-class experiences to virtual learning, Metro district began to collect some very different data. Students were required to "check in" once a day by 6:00 p.m., but school attendance dropped by 25 percent. Students kept forgetting to log in for attendance purposes. Students weren't attending class, or they were present and had their cameras turned off. They did not turn in assignments. No one answered the phone when teachers tried to call the students or their parents.

The teachers became frustrated because they had not been trained in virtual learning techniques. Their class preps took two or three times as long, and teachers felt like they had to be available 24/7. In the Metro district alone, 15 percent of the teaching staff opted for early retirement by mid-year. Staff morale was low, and absenteeism was high: 35 percent of the teaching staff was absent each week —even when teaching virtually. When teachers are absent, students are told to log into another teacher's class and work in that virtual environment for the period or the day.

Other research has revealed that virtual learning prevents children from experiencing socialization. Students with learning difficulties have even more difficulty keeping up with virtual instruction.

**Issue**

Now in 2021, parents are demanding that Dr. Fatimah Williams continue to provide virtual learning opportunities in addition to face-to-face instruction. They want their children to continue with their studies if they cannot attend class in person, whether due to COVID-19, its variations, or other situations, including snow days, family travel, and so on.

The parents point out that in the early part of 2020, students attended school virtually, and the district, in fact, promoted online school. The district provided technology for those who didn't have access to it, and parents found the arrangement convenient.

Parents want a choice. The school board agrees with them.

## Dilemma

Caught between a rock and a hard place, Dr. Fatimah Williams must decide how to lead the district forward. The community and the school board want virtual learning opportunities for their children, in addition to regular face-to-face instruction. Dr. Fatimah Williams knows that virtual learning can be just as effective as in-class instruction, and yet the data that her staff has gathered do not support these research claims:

- Virtual student attendance is 53 percent
- Around 40 percent of students are failing, and
- Around 35 percent of special education students are not meeting their instructional goals.

Additionally, the teachers report being burned out because of having to teach in class and virtually at the same time.

## Questions

1. How should the superintendent proceed? List the steps to be taken and the timeline to take the steps.
2. The data collected by Metro do not align with the meta-analysis conducted by researchers. What does this tell the instructional leaders?
3. What other data do you recommend that Dr. Fatimah Williams look at to make her decision?
4. What options should Dr. Fatimah Williams consider before making her decision?
5. Who else should be involved in making the decision regarding virtual instruction?
6. How should Dr. Fatimah Williams inform the staff and the community of her decision?
7. If you were the incoming superintendent, what would you hope the interim superintendent had done?

## CASE STUDY: BACK TO SCHOOL

Suburban district; Ethics and Professional Norms 2c; Community of Care and Support for Students 5a; Professional Capacity of School Personnel 6h

## Background

Brightly School District is located in a rural community, and it serves approximately 4,000 students in grades Pre-K to 12. The superintendent Tagreed

Jaramillo has closely monitored the spread of COVID-19 in her state, especially in her school district.

Brightly is the largest employer in the community. Many parents look to the schools for information and comprehensive services, whether they want to explore career and college options or learn about health and human services. There have been concerns about spreading COVID-19. Some community members are extremely concerned about the impact of the virus, from the change in how schools have been delivering instruction to how persistent and deadly the virus may be in its spread. Other community members see SARS-CoV-2 as no different from other recent flu strains, citing contradictory advice and data from the CDC and WHO. They believe that developing herd immunity will correct many of the issues associated with the COVID virus.

While reading about COVID-19 in a recent medical study, Superintendent Jaramillo discovered that in public settings where people are confined together for long periods, the virus manifests itself in a variety of ways.

- It exists in 27 percent of exhaled breath samples
- It makes up 4 percent of air samples
- It covers 5 percent of surfaces (hands, mobile phones, computer keyboards), and
- It can be found on 17 percent of toilets and 12.5 percent of floors

Tested door handles were negative for COVID-19.

The study determined that aerosols, not large respiratory droplets or surface areas, are most likely to spread COVID-19.

## Issue

In spring 2020, Brightly District provided virtual instruction for all the students. During this time, class attendance fell from 94 percent to 58 percent. Teachers reported that they were unable to make contact with the absent students. They were overwhelmed, trying to learn how to provide virtual instruction. Grades dropped considerably because of missing assignments, so the district initiated a temporary policy that no child could make less than a 50, and no special education student could make less than a 70 on any assignment or exam.

In fall 2020, the superintendent reopened the Brightly schools for in-person instruction. School attendance rose to 76 percent. Around 100 families withdrew their children for home-schooling until the virus "blows over." The students who returned to classrooms were months behind, and

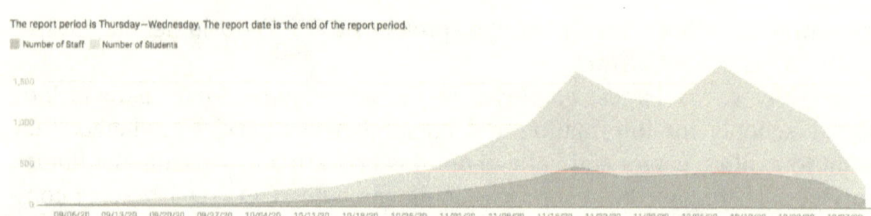

Figure 4.1. Weekly Submissions of Confirmed New Student and Staff COVID-19 Cases

the teachers were frustrated because previous grades had been inflated. To make matters worse, staff absenteeism was at 20 percent. It was nearly impossible to find substitute teachers in the rural district. Most of the certified teachers were retired and older teachers who were concerned about catching COVID.

## Dilemma

With fewer students, a reduced budget, and panicked teachers, Superintendent Tagreed Jaramillo wants to resume quality instruction. She feels that the best way to do that is to get students and teachers to come to school. However, the superintendent has also been watching COVID-19 outbreak trends across her state, as seen in Figure 4.1, which is updated weekly:

Every time students are away from school for a holiday, COVID cases seem to spike upward.

How can Superintendent Tagreed Jaramillo bring the teachers and students back into the buildings for instruction, allay the fears of parents and teachers, and keep everyone safe?

## Questions

1. What protocols must be in place for the safety of students and staff?
2. What kind of communication should Superintendent Tagreed Jaramillo have with her staff about instruction during COVID-19 spread?
3. What kind of communication should Superintendent Tagreed Jaramillo have with the community about instruction during COVID-19 spread?
4. Should students be part of the discussion? Why or why not?
5. How can the superintendent assure parents that the school buildings are safe?
6. If you were the superintendent in Brightly District, what would you do?

# CASE STUDY: SEPARATE BUT EQUAL

Rural district; Community of Care and Support for Students 5b, c

## Background

Superintendent Scott Miller has six campuses in his school district: one high school, two middle schools, and two elementary schools. The sixth campus is under construction, and it is scheduled to open in less than six months. It has been designated as a replacement for one of the elementary schools, the Fordyce campus.

The rural school district of Willis has been growing steadily during the past decade, and the district has built new schools in order to keep up with enrollment. The Fordyce Campus was the district's first elementary school. When the district built its second elementary, Fordyce housed the intermediate grades, and the new campus housed the primary grades.

Fordyce, built some forty years ago, had once been a shining jewel. The superintendent and school board at the time opted for new construction techniques and materials for their first school in the district. The construction company touted the materials and methods as an airtight facility designed for instruction. Rather than use traditional insulation, the school opted for Styrofoam insulation. Styrofoam is extremely resistant to mold, so everyone at the time thought it was a good choice.

Over the years, however, a couple of floods introduced dirt and excessive moisture into the wall spaces, and mold took root. Teachers like to open their classroom windows to catch the cool breezes blowing in from the nearby lake, and in doing so, they introduce mold and mildew spores to the campus.

Eventually, the mold and mildew permeated even the insulation. Teachers and students complained of headaches, and the smell was undeniable.

The only thing to do was move everyone to a new campus.

Of course, that meant figuring out what to do with Fordyce, but Superintendent Miller had an idea. His at-risk population was growing, and many of the kids in high school seemed to bottleneck right at the 10th grade. Many of them needed to work on credit recovery (see table 4.3), and it would be great to have a site where kids could go for extra tutoring help.

Superintendent Miller talked the school board into turning the Fordyce campus into a credit recovery campus. He would staff the campus with a few teachers who would oversee the instructional programming. He would hire one or two teachers with special education certification, and then he planned to have instructional assistants work with students. Hiring teaching assistants would help to keep his operation costs low.

Table 4.3. Credit Recovery Needs in Willis School District

| Enrollment | Brown High School |
|---|---|
|  | 1203 |
| 9th Graders Needing Credit Recovery | 79 |
| 10th Graders Needing Credit Recovery | 188 |
| 11th Graders Needing Credit Recovery | 106 |
| 12th Graders Needing Credit Recovery | 24 |
| % Special Education | 18% |

## Issue

When Fordyce Campus closed and officially reopened, the community was excited initially. A credit recovery center meant that teenagers would be able to catch up and perhaps get ahead in their class work. Their progress would help the district as well, because they would reduce the number of years it might take to graduate. Those in a six-year cohort might graduate in five years, and so on.

Three months after Fordyce reopened, Willis experienced another flood. Torrential rains caused the lake to fill up beyond its capacity, and the water had to go somewhere. Unfortunately, much of it came through Willis. Even the Fordyce campus had water in it, once again.

Crews came and cleaned out the water and the silt, opened the windows and left large blower fans in the rooms to help dry everything out.

Students were back in the building two weeks after that.

## Dilemma

That's when the complaints started again.

The teachers and instructional assistants complained they had headaches so bad that they had to stay home from work. Three of the teachers developed coughs that they couldn't shake. One complained that he couldn't remember things that had recently happened. Substitutes didn't want to take assignments in that building because the word in Willis was that Fordyce was toxic.

The parents thought it was toxic, too. Many of the teens complained of symptoms similar to those of their teachers. One student's parent took the matter seriously and contacted an attorney.

The student, who was in special education, had headaches, coughing, and short-term memory loss. The attorney also made it clear that sending special needs students to an inferior campus known to harbor mold and mildew did not meet the standard of "separate but equal." She pointed out that it appeared that Superintendent Miller had targeted these at-risk kids and sent them to a campus he knew wasn't safe for children. The credit recovery kids had to go to school at the worst campus in the district.

## Questions

1. What's causing the bottleneck at the 10th grade when it comes to credit recovery?
2. Why would the number of students needing credit recovery be lower in the 12th grade?
3. What should Superintendent Miller do about the attorney's claims that he violated "separate but equal" rights for special education students?
4. Is the district liable for the health of the teachers affected by the mold?
5. How can the Fordyce campus be salvaged?

*Chapter 5*

# Cultivating Meaningful Professional Engagement for the Communities We Lead

Superintendents do not work alone, but work in collaboration with school personnel, leadership teams, broader communities, and the Board of Education to ensure a productive school system. That is the focus of this chapter, the professional community that the superintendent oversees, including the teachers and the staff. The responsibilities of the superintendent are many. The superintendent has the task of supervising the general conduct of district schools, developing the instructional curriculum, handling school district management affairs, hiring appropriate personnel, and managing dismissal of personnel based on state policy through the human resources management office. For the local schools, the superintendent seeks ways to encourage the practices of learning communities within the school district for the purpose of working together to improve teaching instructional skills based on the needs of students and if effective will promote higher student learning (Starratt 2017). This chapter focuses on skills and knowledge needed for superintendents, what parents want, value of data, strategic planning, effective communication, learning community practices of ethics and morals, and technology as a resource.

Over the years, the concept evolved into what is commonly referred to as *learning communities* wherein schools are repurposed to support educators' as well as students' learning. This view of schools has been accompanied by a shift in thinking about how educational leaders use professional development as a vehicle for improving teaching and learning. In practice, school- and district-level leaders are positioned as key players in building sustainable learning communities (DuFour 2007), with school leaders creating the internal conditions and district leaders creating the systemic conditions (Fullan 2005). Yet, although district-level superintendents usually hold primary administrative responsibility for school improvement initiatives, the role of district-level superintendents in building capacity for learning communities has not been adequately explored. This gap in the research base was addressed by the study reported in this chapter. Specifically, the chapter presents the findings of a study undertaken to investigate how one group of district-level superintendents studied and understood their role as they participated in their own learning community.

The purpose of professional learning at every level of the organization is to build teacher capacity to teach effectively. Capacity, according to Bruce and Ross (2010), is the "ability to achieve stated goals" (p. 1). In order to achieve the goals, they maintain, teachers need professional learning models that will empower them to engage in meaningful, classroom-embedded inquiry. If district-level school superintendents better understand the essence of authentic learning communities, they may be better equipped to create the conditions within which this sense of empowerment can flourish for all stakeholders. However, superintendents who have not themselves participated in a learning community may have some difficulty with the process. The chapter discussed in this book was undertaken to address meaningful professional engagement.

## CASE STUDY: BUT THEY HAVE A LONG RUNWAY

Urban district; Professional Capacity of School Personnel 5a, c, d

### Background

Namaste Charter School opened its doors as an open-enrollment charter school five years ago. The school began as an elementary school campus with an open concept: no classrooms and no schedules. School staff encouraged students to find their interests and explore them.

When the charter school expanded into the middle school grades two years later, the students still had no classrooms, no schedules, and no bells to remind them what to do next. The same approach was used again this year when Namaste opened its high school.

The students were given "goal sheets" outlining what they needed to know for each grade level. It was their job to make it happen. Some students completed a year's work in far less time than a traditional school year. Others were only halfway into their coursework well after June. Teachers "guided" students in the pursuit of answers rather than tell them. Most of the work at school consisted of independent practice, and students had three to four more hours of it for homework each night.

Table 5.1. Grade-Level Requirement

| | |
|---|---|
| **Exceeds Grade-Level Requirements** | 14% |
| Reading | 21% |
| Mathematics | 7% |
| Science | 9% |
| Social Studies | 13% |
| Writing | 10% |
| **Meets Grade-Level Requirements** | 34% |
| Reading | 52% |
| Mathematics | 19% |
| Science | 31% |
| Social Studies | 37% |
| Writing | 28% |
| **Nearing Grade-Level Requirements** | 68% |
| Reading | 74% |
| Mathematics | 62% |
| Science | 79% |
| Social Studies | 65% |
| Writing | 54% |

"No, it's great, really," said Principal/Superintendent Khadijeh Julius. "For the first time, kids can explore their interests. They are free to do what interests them most."

She was proud of the learning experiences Namaste Charter provided for students. The school's mission is to honor the diversity and knowledge in all students, regardless of their capabilities, background, or any other differences. Around 60 percent of the students are White, and 40 percent are Hispanic.

Mrs. Khadijeh Julius had been hoping that the accountability scores for Namaste would be higher than what they were. The first year, the school had not received an accountability rating because it was new; there was no prior data to compare scores to.

The second and third years were unremarkable. Half the students did well, and half did not. Year four wasn't much different.

All of the teachers meet the requirements for being highly qualified, although some of them have never taught before coming to Namaste High School.

## Issue

The low achievement scores on state assessment have caught the eye of the state. The state agency wants Mrs. Khadijeh Julius and her faculty to identify possible areas of weakness in their instructional plan and its delivery.

Mrs. Khadijeh Julius assured state monitors that the teachers in his school were doing everything they could to teach the students. She herself had seen to their professional development at the beginning of the year by devoting ten days to team building, educational theory, and sessions that showed how to use Namaste's learning management platform.

During each school year, the teachers repeatedly requested for opportunities to attend instructional training at the education service center, as well as other conferences in the area.

"I think teachers need all of their professional development frontloaded at the beginning of the year," she said. "That way teachers don't miss any days of instruction during the rest of the year. They don't need to go to additional training. They can stay in the school building assisting students."

Mrs. Khadijeh Julius refused to change her mind about her professional development plan for teachers, even though she frequently attended trainings and professional development throughout the school year.

## Dilemma

State monitors have advised Mrs. Khadijeh Julius that her approach to providing an education is not working, and she will have to make some transformative changes if she expects the school to stay open.

The monitors strongly suggested revamping the educational approach and providing appropriate professional development to support the teachers in their efforts to improve student achievement.

The teachers want to make the changes, and many of the parents have discussed the necessity of revising the educational approach.

"As much as we love this school building and its original concept," said the PTO president, "it's not working. If our kids can't learn here, we'll re-enroll them in the public school system near us."

## Questions

1. What might account for the low performance in state testing?
2. What flaws does the teacher professional development plan have? How would you change Mrs. Khadijeh Julius's professional development plan for teachers?
3. How can Mrs. Khadijeh Julius work with the state monitors? How can she work with the parents?
4. If you took over Namaste Charter School as its principal/superintendent, what, if any, changes would you make? Why?
5. Should the state have closed the school before now? Why or why not?

## CASE STUDY: SURE SHOTS

Suburban district; Professional Capacity of School Personnel 5g

### Background

Valerie Alexandria is the superintendent of Centerton School District. The student enrollment here consists of 11,000 students. There are multiple high schools, middle schools, and more than a handful of elementary schools.

The community has always been relatively safe, although a few incidents have caused the district to rethink its policy regarding protecting students and employees, especially in the event of a school shooter.

Last year there was a shoot-out at the laundry mat in town. A young male, either drunk or high, tried to rob coins from the washing and drying machines. When the police arrived, the thief pulled out a gun and pointed it at the officers. The thief became Centerton's first fatality of the year.

Centerton had also seen a rise in assaults over the past two years, and domestic violence was on the increase.

For these reasons and more, Superintendent Valerie Alexandria felt like she had to take a stand on safety when it came to the possibility of a school shooting. It seemed like every year there were school shootings across the nation, and it wasn't a matter of *if* but *when* the next one would happen. Superintendent Valerie didn't want Centerton schools to be next on the list.

In looking over the discipline reports from the past three years in her district, Superintendent Valerie noticed the following (see table 5.2):

Table 5.2. Offense

| Offense | 2016 | 2017 | 2018 |
|---|---|---|---|
| Number of Expulsions | 4 | 14 | 35 |
| Number of Weapons (Guns and Knives) Confiscated | 1 | 3 | 8 |
| Alcohol or Drugs | 3 | 11 | 27 |
| Arson | 0 | 0 | 0 |
| Lewd or Indecent Behavior | 17 | 24 | 53 |
| Assault | 4 | 0 | 14 |
| Criminal Mischief | 38 | 32 | 76 |
| Fighting | 39 | 77 | 126 |
| Bullying | 242 | 388 | 492 |

Confiscating weapons and identifying illegal substances required that law enforcement be involved, so each time the campus administrator found something suspicious, he or she called the local police department. The response time to a call placed with 911 took an average of ten minutes.

Superintendent Valerie Alexandria had read that the average contact time between a criminal and a victim was ninety seconds. She was concerned that if a situation got out of control, the damage would be done before the police arrived. Some of the other superintendents in her area suggested taking their approach to the possibility of an active shooter appearing on one of the campuses: tell the teachers to take off their shoes and throw them at the intruders or use wasp spray.

Neither were solutions the superintendent wanted for her schools.

Superintendent Valerie Alexandria reviewed this information, which had recently been released by a national news source.

In the 2019–2020 school year, the federal government reported that there were 235 school shootings (see figures 5.1 and 5.2). But 161 schools or districts reported to a national news source that no school shootings had occurred.

## Issue

Superintendent Valerie Alexandria felt as a thought the district had to move forward on the issue of school safety. She couldn't let another school year go by without addressing basics worries about the well-being of people on campuses.

After meeting with the school board and listening to presentations from security experts, the district opted to install safes in the classrooms. Each safe would contain pepper spray. Only the teacher could unlock the safe and use

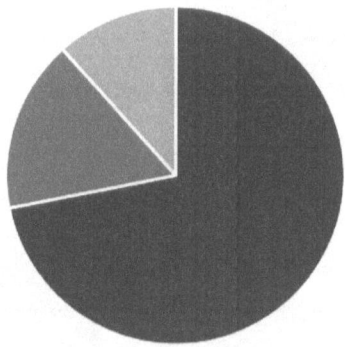

■ School Districts with No Shootings   ■ Cleveland County   ■ Ventura County

**Figure 5.1.   School District Shootings**

## Cultivating Meaningful Professional Engagement

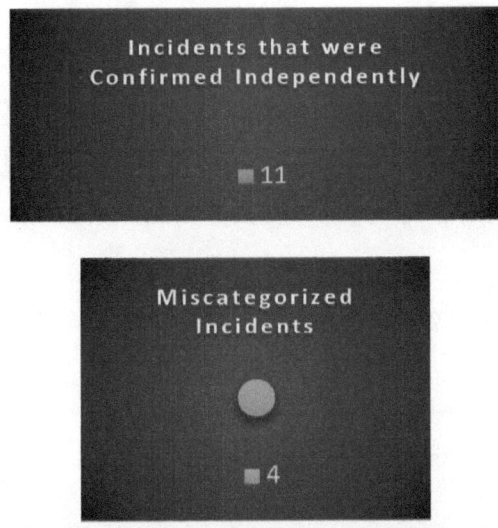

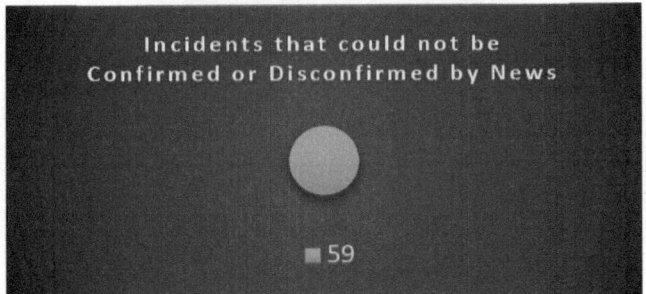

Figure 5.2. Incidents

the spray. The teachers were to receive training at the beginning of the year regarding these new safety measures.

Campus administrators who volunteered to carry a gun would receive extensive training before being allowed to carry it on campus. They had to attend special firearms training with the police force. The district required interested volunteers to pass both annual training and a psychological exam.

Every principal in the district, except two, volunteered to carry a gun.

## Dilemma

During the safety training, one of the high school teachers accidentally deployed a canister of pepper spray. She managed to hit several people in the room with the chemical, and a couple of teachers had to go to the emergency room. Another teacher suffered an asthma attack from the spray.

That wasn't the only problem. One of the middle school principals, Ben Garza, had volunteered to carry a gun on campus. He completed the firearms training with flying colors; he was easily one of the best marksmen on the field. He consistently hit a moving target within the same nine-inch area. Even better, he also used sound judgment in knowing when *not* to fire his weapon.

A second call came into the superintendent's office. It was Alpha Testing Services, the company that the district contracted for the psychological exams.

"I have the test results," said the voice on the other end. "Everyone passed the psych exam, with the exception of one person. One of the middle school principals. Someone named Ben Garza."

## Questions

1. What data are missing? Why do you need it for making your decision?
2. Should superintendent Valerie Alexandria allow teachers to carry guns on campus? Why or why not? How would your answer be different if the school was an elementary? What about an alternative center?
3. What liability does the district have for the teachers who were injured with the pepper spray?
4. What action, if any, should the superintendent take regarding Ben Garza, who failed the psychological exam?

## CASE STUDY: EVALUATION DEVALUATION

Suburban School District; Professional Community for Teachers and Staff 7d, g; Professional Capacity of School Personnel 6a, e

### Background

Superintendent Art Campbell, the leader of the Oceanside School District, has just completed one of the final leadership meetings of the school year. Each department was assigned the principal's tasks that would help them close out the school year and prepare for the upcoming one.

Some of these tasks included determining which students would be retained and which would be promoted, how and where to store the documentation for the year, and of course, getting all of the faculty and staff evaluations and summative assessments finalized and turned in.

Superintendent Campbell was pleased with how well everything had been organized. The meeting ran smoothly, and the principals seem to have no questions or concerns. It was business as usual. And that's just how the superintendent liked it.

Only one week later, however, Superintendent Campbell received a request from three teachers who had been assigned to Danforth Elementary.

Teachers usually did not want to meet with superintendent, so Campbell picked up the phone and called Melissa Atwell, the elementary campus principal. He asked why view teachers might want to meet with him, and why they did not include their principal.

"Beats me," said the principal. "The only thing I can think up is that these three teachers have never really fit in with the other faculty. Maybe they want to see if I can get a transfer."

"You know I don't approve transfers," said the superintendent. "The HR department takes care of all of that."

Superintendent Campbell had time in his schedule, so he decided to listen to the teachers anyway to see what they had to say.

The teachers who come prepared for their meeting brought with them copies of their annual evaluations, as well as a copy of the district evaluation schedule. To the teachers were recommended for nonrenewal. One of them was recommended for a renewal, as long as the contract was probationary.

It was that teacher who spoke up.

"With all respect, sir, my evaluation, as well as these other evaluations, have largely been unfair. The three of us feel as though we could have improved our job performance earlier in the year the principal was looking for."

The teacher went on to explain that he had not been in the evaluation training at the beginning of the year because the human resources department required him to spend additional time reviewing his health care options before making a final insurance determination.

In addition, the teacher did not receive his formal evaluation until April. Principal Atwell conducted the evaluation and promised to get back to him. She did, exactly nineteen working days later. Technically speaking, the principal herself had had no contact with the teacher. Someone had nearly placed his evaluation in his mailbox. The evaluation was not even in a sealed envelope, and when the teacher pulled from its resting place, the pages were rumpled and had coffee stains on them as though someone had rifled through the evaluation.

"And sir," said the teacher, "This sticky note was attached to my evaluation."

He handed the superintendent a 3 × 3 neon-colored paper. It read, "Sign and return."

76                                    Chapter 5

Superintendent Campbell asked the other two teachers if they have had a similar experience. They assured him that they did, holding up their own neon-colored sticky notes with the same words.

The superintendent asked for a moment to look over the three evaluations. In each of them, he noticed frequent references to how well the students performed on their state assessments. The scores had recently been released. And the principal mentioned specific passing percentages for both subject areas and student subpopulations. For all of the teachers, she recommended, "Learn how to meet student needs and help them achieve in reaching their goals." She closed teacher evaluation with the words, "Thanks for all your hard work this year."

Superintendent Campbell looked up from the three evaluations.

"What would you like to see happen?" he asked.

Each teacher had a different response: The first teacher said, "I'd like to be transferred to another campus." The second teacher said, "I'd like another evaluation from an impartial observer."

The third teacher said, "I would like those things as well, but I would also like the principal to follow the schedule that the school district set forth. If I had known that there were challenges earlier in the year, I could have addressed them, and been a better teacher because of it. Now I feel like my work has been tossed aside, as though what I have done has had no impact throughout the school year."

**Issue**

The evaluations performed by several of the camp administrators in Oceanside cool district have often been completed incorrectly, turned in past the deadlines, and in general, have not followed the protocol set forth by the state and the district itself.

Just how large of a problem teacher evaluation compliance is has been difficult to determine because for the past several years, no one has monitored the principals' work in evaluating their faculties.

It has come to the superintendent's attention, however, that one principal in particular, has not followed the evaluation protocol.

**Dilemma**

Three teachers from the Danforth Elementary, where Melissa Atwell has been the principal for the past eight years, have come forward with a complaint regarding their annual evaluations.

Their claim states that principal Atwell has refused to follow agreed-upon deadlines for conducting teacher evaluations and providing feedback in a timely fashion. In addition, she routinely waits until the end of the year to complete the evaluations so that she can consider state assessment scores as part of each teacher's summative evaluation.

Superintendent Campbell has been unaware of the problem until now.

## Questions

1. Whose job is it to monitor how well the principals evaluate their teaching staff and whether or not they are in compliance with timelines?
2. Why is it a good idea to ask, "What would you like to see happen?"
3. Should the superintendent approve the transfer requests or overturn the evaluations and decisions regarding contract renewal? Why or why not?
4. How legal is it to include state assessment scores in the teacher evaluation? Should they be included or excluded?
5. What should the superintendent's response be if the teachers decide to get their unions and involved in the evaluation devaluation case?

## CASE STUDY: MORE THAN MONEY

Rural district; Meaningful Engagement of Families and Community 8h, i

## Background

Like many other superintendents in her state, Dr. Lisa Bentley is feeling the pains of not having enough funding for school programs and initiatives. The Meadow School District has always offered a diversified curriculum. Students took classes in a variety of fields, and they had ample opportunities to gain new experiences.

Meadow School District had a rigorous curriculum consisting of opportunities to earn dual credit, learn a foreign language, play sports, and engage in the arts. Students also had a wide range of extra-curricular clubs from which to choose.

All of that was coming to an end.

Once again, the state education agency announced imminent cutbacks in funding. The rural districts would likely be hit the hardest since they received less in taxes and federal funding.

Meadow School District receives approximately $1.5 million in Title I funding, and it receives less than $15,000 in for bilingual/ESL funding.

Other funding cuts included:

a. Local     +2 percent
b. State cuts     −3 percent

c. Federal
d. Title I              −7 percent
e. Technology           −14 percent
f. Special Education    +4 percent

Dr. Bentley has served on a steering committee consisting of superintendents and businesspeople across the state. They have been meeting for the last year to discuss the issues facing schools, including cost of living expenses, inflation, and reductions in formula funding. As frustrating as it was to see financial support shrivel up, the committee felt energized because they were exploring new options with open minds.

Some of the options included increasing sales tax, initiating a variety of property tax algorithms, and floating bonds to carry the districts further down the road.

Several committee members, including Dr. Bentley, have been of the opinion that increasing state funding by a mere $1 per pupil will increase the property values of the residents in their communities by at least $20.

"For every dollar we get," said Dr. Bentley, "we make $19. The investment in education has always been well spent. It always will be. Students get an education, and our communities are rewarded as well."

With all the work that had been done, the steering committee had still not been able to take a resolution to their state legislators.

## Issue

Even though Dr. Bentley is an ardent advocate of exploring alternative education funding, she and her peers have not been able to come up with a solution that would satisfy most stakeholders when it comes to financing education.

Once again, another school year is starting, and Dr. Bentley must decide where the money will do the best for the students in the Meadow School District.

In looking over the projections, she decided to eliminate some of the instructional positions first. Her proposal includes eliminating the position of reading specialist at the elementary school. She also wants to eliminate the four librarian positions in the district. To staff the library, Dr. Bentley wants to hire an instructional assistant to serve in this capacity, and the assistant will rotate to a campus each day of the week.

In addition, Dr. Bentley has decided that eliminating all of the art classes except for those required for high school credit will free up more money in the way of salaries, supplies, and space.

The last change Dr. Bentley will propose to the school board is to eliminate most after-school activities that require paying additional stipends to teachers. Doing away with these activities will also eliminate the need for additional transportation services.

She had a few other suggestions to bring up at the board meeting.

## Dilemma

Dr. Bentley prepared her proposals for the June board meeting. She had talked individually to several board members, revealing that she had come up with a money-saving plan for the district. Each member was in favor of saving money, although they didn't know just yet how it would happen.

When Dr. Bentley's administrative assistant typed up the agenda and the proposals, the part about eliminating the librarian positions caught her eye. Her husband was the middle school librarian.

By the time the school board settled into their seats for their meeting, the board room was packed with concerned parents and employees. Some of them had already signed up for discussion time at the beginning of the meeting.

They were already talking among themselves about the apparent lack of transparency and certain inefficiency.

## Questions

1. How serious are the budget cuts? What kind of impact might they have on the district?
2. How should Dr. Bentley have handled her suggestions for saving money? Who should have been involved and why?
3. What are some ways the district could generate funding or reduce spending? Toss out as many ideas as possible, if even they sound crazy at first.
4. Would cutting programs save money? How should Dr. Bentley go about cutting some of the school district's programs?

## CASE STUDY: BONDING WITH THE COMMUNITY

Suburban district; Meaningful Engagement of Families and Community 8g, h

## Background

Jack Jacobs had been the superintendent of the Las Salle Public Schools for eight years, right at the height of exponential growth in what was once a sleepy little town.

## Chapter 5

LaSalle had always been a small community, one that resisted change and liked things the way they once were. For that reason, many people fleeing urban areas in search of a better life came to La Salle. It was peaceful—a real slice of Americana.

The school superintendent, Jack Jacobs, adored the town the moment he saw it. There was a quaint town square, and tourists flocked to it on the weekends. The people who lived in La Salle looked out after each other, and they took pride in their community and their schools.

"I could retire a happy man here," thought Jacobs. He jumped at the chance to lead the district when the school board offered him the top position.

"We want someone who will be here for the long haul," said the board president. "Someone who truly wants to be part of our community."

"That's me," said Jacobs.

Superintendent Jacobs had a vision for the district. He knew that one day the district would no longer be a small town. It would grow into a prestigious community nestled in the suburbs.

In his role as the superintendent of La Salle schools, Jack Jacobs managed to get two bonds passed so far. The first was for a new elementary school, and it was $9.5 million. The second bond had a price tag of $27.2 million, and it would pay for repairs to existing buildings and update the athletic facilities.

Now Superintendent Jacobs wanted to get a third bond passed. The price tag for this one? $48.8 million. Some of the larger projects include:

- Building a new elementary school. Cost: $33 million.
- Renovating the oldest campus in the district and turning it into an alternative campus. Cost: $1 million.
- Digital marquees at the high school, middle school, and central administration buildings. Cost: $150,000.
- Renovations to existing schools. Cost: $12 million
- Purchase of new vehicles for district use, including trucks with lift gates and transportation for the superintendent. Cost: $100,000
- Classroom cameras for security at each of the campuses. Cost: $250,000.
- Renovations to the athletic facilities. Cost: $1.25 million.
- Project management costs. Cost: $1.5 million.
- Purchase of handheld technology devices for students. Costs: $950,000.

Jacobs directed the district IT department to set up a dedicated page on the district website. It was exclusively for distributing information and updates about the bonds.

Superintendent Jacobs also sent a letter to parents in the community that read, in part:

Our current elementary classrooms no longer meet minimum standards for minimum square footage. They are less than 650 square feet in size, and the new standard for a classroom of 25 students is 750 square feet. We must build a new elementary school that can accommodate the greater enrollment.

La Salle School District currently accepts transfer students, but these facilities are not being built for them. We need the new school and the upgrades regardless of whether we accept transfer students or not.

Our new proposed school site will require major site work, including the redesigning of traffic flow on the main roads around the school. A Land Feasibility Study determined that this tract is the best site for a school; even the costs are greater than at any other proposed site.

Should you have any questions or concerns, please contact at one of the numbers below.

## Issue

Not everyone is a fan of another bond package in La Salle. Taxes had been climbing steadily because of the influx of new residents.

La Salle has a divided population: half of the households are families with children, and half are retired people on relatively fixed incomes. The families wanted the bond to pass. It would mean improved facilities and programs for their kids. They didn't mind paying a little extra in their taxes for that. If things got really bad, they could always move again.

The retirees did not want their taxes to go up, and they worried that if a large population moved out of La Salle and into one of the neighboring districts to pay less in taxes, who would be left holding the checkbook?

After researching the bonds, residents discovered that neither bond was insured, and there was no discussion of the third being insured, either.

The discontent was low key at first, but as the election neared, residents became more vocal about the bond.

## Dilemma

The community has become highly divided over the proposed bond. Many of the residents want to do everything they can to improve the school facilities for the children here. Some are opposed to any kind of bond. Then there are a handful of residents who while understanding a bond may be inevitable, also disagree with some of the items being considered.

There was also talk that this was Superintendent Jacobs's last year in education. He reached retirement age two years ago, and he could leave the district at any time, retiring comfortably. There was fear that he would leave the district altogether, but only after strapping La Salle with $100 million in debt.

"There's no way you'll get another bond passed here in La Salle," said the mayor. "I personally will see to it that your pet projects do not get funded."

Jack Jacobs knew that a new bond was the only way the district would be able to keep up with the tiny town's growth. It was also a way to poise the district for future growth. They might even name a school after him one day.

He had to get the bond passed if the district was going to keep up with the other districts in the area.

## Questions

1. Is it a good idea to post updates on the school website about the current and proposed bonds? Why or why not?
2. What is the benefit of securing funding through bonds?
3. What items in the third bond package could be questionable?
4. Should school bonds be insured? Why or why not?
5. How should the superintendent go about generating interest and support for the next bond?

*Chapter 6*

# Supporting Sustainable School Improvement

Since the passage of the No Child Left Behind Act of 2001 (NCLB), renewed emphasis has been placed on school accountability. With this renewed emphasis, school superintendents have been focusing on gains in student achievement and therefore this is the focus of this chapter. Cambron-McCabe et al. (2005) stated that regardless of how NCLB develops, schools will sooner or later be judged on their ability to close the achievement gap. They continued by stating that this gap is often defined in racial terms, because so many minority students are from low-income families, but the gap is more likely to be a consequence of income and social class than of race or ethnicity. Bernhardt (2004) summarized the school improvement process as a mechanism that uses a systematic approach to help school close the achievement gap for all students. Therefore, schools need to recharge the school improvement process within their school buildings.

With increased pressure for accountability, superintendents search for systemic processes that impact student learning. Bonney 2015 stated that the district accreditation process embraces a systems approach because it is designed as a systemic process that examines how all elements of a school district work together to impact results connected to student learning. All parts of the district are required to focus on a shared vision and goals for improvement, align operations to achieve a shared vision and goals, and connect improvement efforts to maximize results. To achieve this requirement, districts are expected to not only meet the accreditation standard for quality systems but also to identify and guide the implementation of a systemic continuous improvement process.

The school improvement cycle within a school district provides the structure and framework for continuous improvement. It provides for continued gains in student achievement, hence accountability. Educational leaders need to understand the phases associated with the school improvement cycle in order for the process to be successful. In fact, "almost every school in America today is or was in the process of 'restructuring.' However, a large percentage of these schools will abandon their efforts before they complete their restructuring process" (Bernhardt 1999, 1). The challenge today is to determine why school superintendents are failing to complete the cycle and avoiding gains in student achievement. According to Chenoweth 2021, several recent research studies of school districts that have significantly improved levels of student achievement converge on a critical finding, an effective superintendent was identified as key to the success of improvement efforts. Bernhardt (1999) stated that the systematic school improvement process serves as a means to improve student results. In fact, Marx (2006) predicted that a trend of continuous improvement will replace quick fixes and defense of the status quo. As a result of this research, then the focus of this chapter is on continuous school improvement.

## CASE STUDY: BE MY GUEST

Rural district; Operations and Management 9d

### Background

Superintendent Roberta White asked her curriculum director to oversee the adoption of the new English language textbooks for the district.

This new adoption is a critical event for the district. The textbooks currently in adoption have been in use for nine years, and they are not only out of date, but they are well used. Whatever textbook the district adopts for English reading and writing will be in use for the next ten years.

The district is in its second year of poor performance in reading and writing (see table 6.1). Mrs. White has repeatedly told Curriculum Director Betty Brown that the scores must come up. This will be Ms. Brown's last year

Table 6.1. Summerville School District Reading and Writing Scores

| Subject | 2019 | 2020 |
|---|---|---|
| Reading | 64% | 52% |
| Writing | 56% | 58% |

with the district if there no improvement in reading and writing as seen in the assessment scores at the end of the year. Ms. Brown's contract will not be renewed.

Mrs. White has sat through several of the presentations by the textbook companies, and she was particularly impressed with the materials from ABC Publishers. ABC offers a comprehensive package that includes the following:

- textbooks,
- leveled readers for elementary students,
- online portfolio/video/interactive lesson access,
- three years of free tech support with an option to purchase more, and
- professional development for teachers.

ABC is well known in the textbook industry because it's a big company with deep pockets. The other publishers who are presenting their materials include Summit and Acme Publishers. They are smaller companies that are trying to compete with ABC.

Mrs. Brown likes Acme Publishers' materials the best. Certainly, it's important that they are aligned to the standards teachers must meet (see table 6.2). The decision would be left to a vote from the ELA teachers in the district.

## Issue

Ben Smiley is the ABC rep. He wants to make this sale to the district, and he's prepared to lock it in place, doing (nearly) anything to get it.

Table 6.2. Summerville School District Analysis of Textbook Alignment to Standards and Needs

| Alignment | ABC | Acme | Summit |
|---|---|---|---|
| **Reading Standards** | ✓ | ✓ | |
| **Writing Standards** | | ✓ | ✓ |
| **Professional Development** | ✓ | ✓ | |
| **Tech Support** | ✓ | | ✓ |
| **Student Friendly** | ✓ | ✓ | |
| **Teacher Friendly** | ✓ | ✓ | ✓ |
| **Additional Costs to District** | $$$ | $ | $$ |

He's already taken Mrs. White out to lunch several times, paying for her lunches, and he's tried to do the same for the curriculum director. She has turned him down each time, saying that because this is a rural community, it's inappropriate for her to eat lunch alone with him.

Changing his tactics, Ben offered Mrs. Brown tickets to an amusement park in a nearby city. He knew she wanted to take her five children for a mini-vacation, and because the park is two-and-a-half hours away, Ben said, "Let me cover two nights for your hotel, too."

Mrs. Brown accepted his offer, but she told him, "There's no guarantee how the vote will go. It's completely up to the teachers."

"I know," he said.

## Dilemma

When she came back from her mini-vacation as a guest of ABC Publishing, Mrs. Brown conducted the textbook vote with the English teachers for the adoption of the new textbook. She carefully explained the benefits and drawbacks each publisher offered.

The vote results were as follows:

- ABC      30 percent
- Acme     30 percent
- Summit   40 percent

Superintendent White was already on the phone, wanting to know what textbook the teachers recommended. She hoped they chose her favorite, ABC. Ben was such a nice person to work with.

Mrs. Brown told Mrs. White that Acme won the vote. Clearly it was the best choice because it was the most aligned. The materials should help teachers improve student performance.

"I can't describe my disappointment," said Mrs. White. "I certainly hope you know what you're doing. If you don't, it's your last year here."

## Questions

1. Was Mrs. Brown justified in making her decision? Why or why not?
2. Would it be appropriate for the superintendent to ask to see the results of the vote?
3. Should Mrs. White have told Mrs. Brown that her job is on the line?
4. What should Mrs. White do or say about the vacation provided by ABC?
5. Which textbook company would you have picked, and why?

## CASE STUDY: CONTINUOUS IMPROVEMENT BEGINS HERE

Suburban district; School Improvement 10c, d

### Background

Mahmoud Gilmore is the superintendent of the Ballentine Public School District. He recently received the accountability scores for Ballentine. The district-wide average in reading was an 83, and mathematics was a 67.

The superintendent Dr. Mahmoud Gilmore had a mixed response to what he saw before him.

The year before, Ballentine Public Schools earned a 78 in reading and a 71 in mathematics. The year before that, the reading average was a 72, and the mathematics score was an 81. Each year since he took over the district, the superintendent saw a steady increase in reading scores and an equally steady decline in math scores.

At the urging of the curriculum director, the superintendent, Dr. Mahmoud Gilmore, agreed to try out a new computer-based reading program across the district. The program identified areas of weakness for every student, established reading pathways for students, and it provided adaptive instruction each step of the way.

At first, the reading teachers complained that the program was taking the place of reading instruction. Three years later, they have seen the benefit of computer-assisted instruction (CAI).

Parents, too, were against the adoption of the CAI program. Many of them wanted to know about real reading; after all, why else have a library if no one was going to read the books from it? Over time, they saw not only an improvement in their children's scores but also a greater appreciation for reading. Children not formerly identified as avid readers were checking out books from the library.

The district had not, however, fared so well in mathematics. Three years ago the scores were much higher. Every year since Superintendent Gilmore came to the district, the math scores dropped.

Superintendent Mahmoud Gilmore wondered how well the other districts in his area fared in reading and mathematics. He asked his director of assessment and accountability to see how well the other districts performed on the accountability assessments.

He received the following (see table 6.3):

*State Accountability Scores by District and Subpopulation*

**Table 6.3. Assessment Scores**

| Assessment Scores | Applewhite | Ballentine | Churchton | Dandelion | Exeter |
|---|---|---|---|---|---|
| **Reading (R)** | 79 | 83 | 88 | 86 | 74 |
| **Math (M)** | 75 | 67 | 65 | 81 | 59 |
| **Enrollment** | 11,321 | 14,456 | 8,793 | 16,547 | 19,654 |
| **Gender** | | | | | |
| Female—R | 84 | 89 | 82 | 85 | 80 |
| Female—M | 72 | 79 | 64 | 82 | 62 |
| Male—R | 72 | 62 | 74 | 83 | 48 |
| Male—M | 78 | 54 | 67 | 85 | 54 |
| Gender Neutral—R | — | 58 | — | — | 73 |
| Gender Neutral—M | — | 52 | — | — | 36 |
| **Race/Ethnicity** | | | | | |
| African American—R | 78 | 81 | 78 | 80 | 65 |
| African American—M | 76 | 60 | 62 | 75 | 57 |
| Hispanic—R | 67 | 82 | 82 | 77 | 68 |
| Hispanic—M | 72 | 61 | 78 | 76 | 56 |
| White—R | 83 | 84 | 90 | 89 | 82 |
| White—M | 84 | 69 | 75 | 87 | 80 |
| Native American—R | — | — | — | 78 | — |
| Native American—M | — | — | — | 73 | — |
| Pacific Islander/Asian—R | 86 | — | — | — | — |
| Pacific Islander/Asian—M | 90 | — | — | — | — |
| **Special Populations** | | | | | |
| Gifted—R | 86 | 92 | 93 | 95 | 90 |
| Gifted—M | 84 | 87 | 83 | 91 | 87 |
| Special education—R | 64 | 68 | 79 | 75 | 66 |
| Special education—M | 59 | 65 | 60 | 73 | 51 |
| Bilingual/ELL—R | 55 | 84 | 80 | 77 | 65 |
| Bilingual/ELL—M | 67 | 64 | 76 | 76 | 55 |
| Migrant—R | 68 | 85 | 84 | 71 | — |
| Migrant—M | 70 | 63 | 77 | 72 | — |
| At-risk—R | 58 | 79 | 76 | 72 | 65 |
| At-risk—M | 72 | 69 | 69 | 66 | 55 |
| Homeless—R | — | 65 | — | 56 | — |
| Homeless—M | — | 61 | — | 48 | — |

## Issue

Superintendent Mahmoud Gilmore wanted to share the scores with the administrators and the teachers across the district.

He planned to meet first with the administrators to celebrate the campus successes and identify what might be causing the low math scores. From there, the campus principals would take the data back to their campuses and review them with their teachers.

Superintendent Mahmoud Gilmore suspected there would be little to no reason to change the reading program, but instruction in mathematics needed immediate intervention.

Most importantly, the superintendent wanted to show how the campus teams in his district were performing compared to those in other districts in the area.

## Dilemma

At the administrative meeting, Superintendent Gilmore asked the principals to sit in their feeder-school groups. The elementary schools that fed into the middle schools and the middle schools that fed into the high schools would sit together.

As the superintendent began sharing the information, one of the principals turned to another one in her feeder-school group and said, "I know how we can raise scores in math. Replace this elementary principal with one who knows what she's doing."

Superintendent Mahmoud Gilmore cleared his throat. He needed to explain his plan for data analysis so the administrators could help to find a solution.

## Questions

1. What plan for data analysis should the superintendent outline for the campus administrators?
2. Should the administrators at Ballantine be more concerned about subpopulations or the subjects? Why?
3. Would you recommend contacting any of the other districts to see how they are improving scores? Why or why not?
4. What, if anything, should the superintendent tell the principal who accused the elementary principal of not knowing how to do her job?
5. How can the analysis be useful for teachers back at each campus?
6. At what point should the superintendent and the administrators bring parents and students into the conversation about performance on the state accountability assessments?

## CASE STUDY: READING BETWEEN THE LINES

Suburban district; School Improvement 10e

## Background

Superintendent Mac Gilmore received the most recent accountability scores for his district. As expected, the reading scores were up. The Ballantine Public School District committed three years ago to implement a new computer-assisted reading program, and it seemed to be working.

They needed a similar miracle for the math scores, which had been falling every year for the past three years.

When the superintendent met with the principals, he allowed them time within their feeder groups to reflect on the data and compare their performance to the other nearby districts. The activity had been well received, although there was one altercation; the superintendent handled the matter in private by asking the experienced principal to help the new administrator instead of bullying her.

At the meeting, the administrative team requested a breakdown of the scores by grade level, and they received it (see table 6.4). They wanted to pinpoint any areas of difficulty before meeting with their teachers.

In addition, they were curious about the experience levels of their teaching staff, and how they compared to the other districts as well (see table 6.5).

## Issue

Superintendent Gilmore plans to continue his work with the campus administrators and teachers to improve student performance not only in reading but especially in mathematics. The principals want to focus their efforts on 4th- and 7th-grade mathematics, because these two areas earned

Table 6.4. Assessment Scores by Grade Level

| Assessment Scores | Applewhite | Ballentine | Churchton | Dandelion | Exeter |
|---|---|---|---|---|---|
| **Reading Average** | 79 | 83 | 88 | 86 | 74 |
| 3 | 75 | 85 | 91 | 88 | 72 |
| 4 | 85 | 71 | 90 | 89 | 71 |
| 5 | 82 | 75 | 88 | 90 | 76 |
| 6 | 76 | 77 | 89 | 86 | 74 |
| 7 | 73 | 69 | 83 | 82 | 65 |
| 8 | 81 | 80 | 84 | 87 | 67 |
| 9 | 75 | 84 | 82 | 85 | 75 |
| 10 | 72 | 82 | 83 | 86 | 77 |
| 11 | 74 | 80 | 80 | 85 | 75 |
| **Math Average** | 75 | 67 | 65 | 81 | 59 |
| 3 | 78 | 79 | 65 | 89 | 74 |
| 4 | 75 | 74 | 64 | 78 | 72 |
| 5 | 80 | 76 | 66 | 90 | 73 |
| 6 | 79 | 75 | 67 | 88 | 71 |
| 7 | 70 | 56 | 60 | 75 | 51 |
| 8 | 72 | 63 | 64 | 82 | 58 |
| 9 | 74 | 67 | 65 | 81 | 55 |
| 10 | 73 | 70 | 67 | 81 | 53 |
| 11 | 75 | 72 | 65 | 82 | 60 |

Table 6.5. Percentage of Teachers

| % of Teachers | Applewhite | Ballentine | Churchton | Dandelion | Exeter |
|---|---|---|---|---|---|
| 0–1 Yrs. Experience | 10 | 30 | 15 | 20 | 0 |
| 2–5 Yrs. Experience | 15 | 20 | 20 | 10 | 5 |
| 5–10 Yrs. Experience | 25 | 25 | 35 | 20 | 5 |
| 11–15 Yrs. Experience | 30 | 10 | 20 | 25 | 10 |
| 16–20 Yrs. Experience | 10 | 10 | 5 | 20 | 15 |
| 20+ Yrs. Experience | 10 | 5 | 5 | 5 | 65 |

the lowest scores. Three out of four other districts are experiencing similar problems.

## Dilemma

The principals want to send their math teachers to Applewhite, Ballentine, and Exeter Public Schools to see why they are having similar problems in 4th and 7th grades. The principals think that if their teachers confer with other teachers about the challenge, they may be able to come up with a solution and reverse the trend.

The superintendent disagrees. He wants the campus to focus on 3rd and 6th grades first, and then have those teachers move with their students to the next grade level.

The human resources director insists that the reason the scores are so low—and sinking farther—in mathematics is that the district has a large percentage of teachers who are new to the profession. Around 30 percent of the faculty has one or fewer years of experience.

## Questions

1. What can be learned by comparing grade-level performance across districts?
2. Is the real issue the instructional alignment, student discipline, and off-task behavior, or having a large number of novice teachers in the district? How could you tell?
3. Is it better to have a new mathematics program or provide professional development for the math teachers? Explain your answer.
4. What situationally appropriate strategies for improvement would you recommend? Why?
5. If you were the superintendent, where would you recommend beginning your strategies? Why?
6. How long should the superintendent wait to see growth?

## CASE STUDY: WHAT'S IN A GRADE?

Rural district; School Improvement 10d, e

**Background**

Principals complained when one of the metrics used for campus success was the number of As, Bs, and so on. If not that, then use what? What about grading notebooks and organization?

What about participation?

When Elda Ortiz became the superintendent at Jefferson School District, she knew she would have to guide the board and the schools through some significant changes to improve student achievement.

Students scored an average 189 points on their standardized tests in math, and they scored an average of 276 on their reading exam. The highest possible score was 500. The students in Jefferson scored in the 40th percentile, on average, which was lower when compared with their peers across the nation.

To make matters worse, when Superintendent Ortiz looked at student growth, the students were regressing by 12 percent every year in math, and 5 percent in reading.

The community at large was proud of the Jefferson schools, and they sported "Honor Roll" bumper stickers on their cars and trucks. It seemed like almost everyone in the district had been on the Honor Roll at some point.

Grades at Jefferson were a source of pride. The previous superintendent made them a priority, telling administrators at the campuses, "No child fails." The principals, in turn, told their teachers that no child fails. The mantra quickly became the district's mission.

Teachers included participation grades, which made up 25 percent of the final grade. The teachers also required subject notebooks. Students had to organize all their notes and assignments for each six weeks, and the notebooks counted for 25 percent of the grade.

Any time the teacher who assigned failing grades to a student had to meet with an administrator and show what effort they made to work with the student. Teachers had to prove they worked with the failing student beyond the standard class time, whether that was during lunch, before or after school, or on weekends. In addition, there had to be at least three contacts made with the parents and samples of student work.

To give students every possible opportunity to make excellent grades, the former superintendent initiated a new policy that allowed students to turn in assignments any time—right up until grades were due to run the report cards. No re-teach was necessary, and students could resubmit homework, essays, and even tests.

As a result, the last week of the six weeks was always hurried. Teachers either showed movies in class or gave easy assignments so they could get as much grading done during the day as possible. It was common knowledge that little to no teaching took place during that last week.

Students nearly always made excellent grades, as indicated by last year's summary report (see table 6.6):

Table 6.6. Grade Reporting from the Previous School Year

| Student Category | Semester A | Semester B |
|---|---|---|
| % of Students on A Honor Roll | 23 | 16 |
| % of Students on A/B Honor Roll | 34 | 28 |
| % of Students on B Honor Roll | 31 | 25 |
| % of Students Making at least 1 C | 47 | 59 |
| % of Students Making at least 1 D | 22 | 31 |
| % of Students Making at least 1 F | 13 | 19 |
| % of Students with C Average | 10 | 21 |
| % of Students with D Average | 2 | 6 |
| % of Students with F Average | 1 | 4 |

## Issue

The prior practice of "no child fails" became so ingrained in the culture of the district that the teachers found it easier to accept assignment revisions than prove that they tried to re-teach their students.

Students were losing nearly six weeks of instruction every year because teachers were taking class time to catch up on grading. As a result, students were losing ground each year in math and reading, as indicated by standardized test scores.

The students and parents were lulled into a false sense of academic comfort; they thought everything was fine because no child failed. The grades did not reflect student achievement or performance. Only half of the grade came from mastery of the learning standards. The other half came from participation and organization skills.

## Dilemma

Many policies had to change in the district. First, Superintendent Ortiz would have to change the mission statement because "no child fails" had morphed into something different than intended. The schools would need new grading policies, and most importantly, the students required intervention.

Superintendent Ortiz wanted to initiate after-school tutoring and make summer school mandatory for some of the students needing additional help; angry parents came forward.

They complained that their children had always made excellent grades. They wanted to know why the district wanted to require additional instructional time. It seemed unfair that suddenly students would have to stay after school. The parents of high school–age students pointed out that if their kids had to attend summer school, they couldn't have summer jobs.

Furthermore, why were students doing so poorly with standardized testing if the teachers are giving As and Bs? Didn't the teachers know what they were doing?

## Questions

1. What issue exists when grades alone become the indicator of success?
2. Should participation and organizational skills be part of student grades? If so, how much of the grade should be based on content mastery? What policy changes should be made, and how should the superintendent prioritize them?
3. Who should be a part of making recommendations for these changes?
4. What new data measure should the district focus on to measure student success?
5. What would you tell the parents if you were Superintendent Ortiz?

## CASE STUDY: SOCIAL MEDIA THREAT

Urban district; School Improvement 10h, i

## Background

Dr. Aymen Lane is the superintendent of Randolph Heights Public School District. He's held this position for several years, and during this time, the use of social media has become a concern because it has seemed to preoccupy many people's time and too much of his time and focus.

The district has had a long-standing policy that teachers cannot friend their students on social platforms. The district policy discourages teachers and administrators from friending each other and posting about work conditions.

The district has had a much harder time keeping track of student posts on social media, but felt as though it had a duty to monitor conservations among students to protect the interests of the district as well as the safety of students (see figure 6.1 and table 6.7).

At the beginning of the school year, the district hired a data company to monitor the social media accounts of students and employees. Specifically, the company looked for any indication of improper relationships between teachers and students, teachers and administrators, and other references for concern, including references to suicide, cyberbullying, and violence.

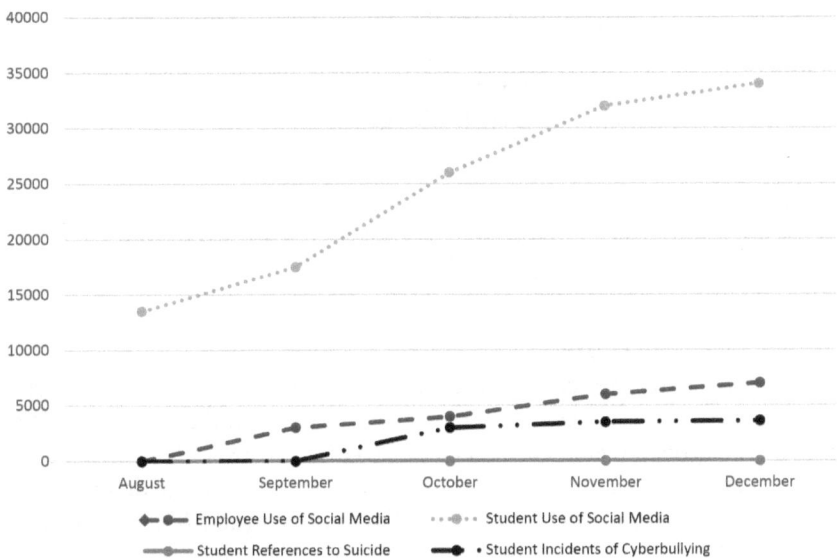

**Figure 6.1.** Social Media Use in Randolph Heights School District

**Table 6.7.** Social Media Use in Randolph Heights School District

| District Social Media Use BM | August | September | October | November | December |
|---|---|---|---|---|---|
| Employee Use of Social Media | 521 | 1569 | 3512 | 5468 | 6159 |
| Student Use of Social Media | 12047 | 17845 | 26593 | 31250 | 33456 |
| Student References to Suicide | 7 | 24 | 51 | 123 | 189 |
| Student Incidents of Cyberbullying | 75 | 217 | 1143 | 1864 | 2587 |
| Student Attempts to Incite Violence | 12 | 43 | 137 | 226 | 323 |

Superintendent Aymen Lane received a preliminary data report called *Social Media Use in Randolph Heights School District*.

## Issue

When Superintendent Aymen Lane looked at the report, he noticed an increase in posting as the semester progressed. Both employees and students were posting more on social media each month.

Perhaps the most alarming part of the report was that the number of threats was steadily increasing. Comments about suicide increased sevenfold. Cyberbullying was becoming more common, and so were attempts to incite violence and create disruption.

Now that the Dr. Aymen Lane had this information, he felt compelled to take action, so he planned to have a meeting with his senior administrative team and the school building administrators to review the data and decide upon what to do next. He scheduled the meeting right after the holiday break between semesters.

## Dilemma

During the holidays, one of the students in the Randolph Heights Public School District committed suicide by hanging himself. He was home alone the day it happened, and his parents did not discover what he had done until they came home from work.

The student had repeatedly been cyberbullied on social media, and the problem grew worse and worse. The parents were unaware of the growing problem on their son's social media accounts, but two of his teachers had friended him. One teacher, Mrs. Dakota, urged him to talk to his parents or call a crisis hotline, and she posted the phone number. The other teacher, Mr. Caroline, said nothing.

The social media monitoring software used by the school district reported references anonymously. The software did not identify individuals or individual incidents.

## Questions

1. Should the district change its policy regarding teachers' and administrators' use of social media? Why or why not?
2. Does the district have a right or a duty to monitor students, to protect itself, and to protect student safety?
3. What other data does the superintendent need to make a recommendation or take action?
4. What recommendation or action should the Dr. Aymen Lane take? Why?
5. Should the district have stepped in sooner to prevent the suicide? What responsibility do the teachers have?
6. If you were the superintendent in Randolph Heights, what would you recommend that the superintendent work on first: suicide prevention, cyberbullying, or inciting violence? Why?

# Appendix A: Possible Resolutions

**RESOLUTIONS**

Case Studies in the same order that they appear in the book.

## Chapter One: Our Mission, Vision, and Values Encompass Who We Are

*Case Study: The Trauma-Informed Care Initiative*

Suburban district; Professional Community for Teachers and Staff 7b; School Improvement 5a

Dr. Hana Jackson would do well to review data by subpopulations to ensure that no special population is more favored or disenfranchised than another. For example, are boys or girls more likely to have EBD episodes? Is one race more predisposed to behavior malfunction than another? What would cause these disparities?

According to the research, management and teacher gender have the greatest impact on classroom behavior. Dr. Jackson should focus on these two significant areas to improve student behavior. Teachers should be given the opportunity to learn and develop trauma-informed care strategies to help students manage their behaviors in the classroom.

The district could encourage the teachers to take the lead in this initiative. The campus administrators should support the work of the teachers, and Dr. Hana Jackson should support their work.

If Dr. Hana Jackson asks the principals to manipulate the discipline data, the principals can and should confront her professionally. They can make a formal complaint against her to the school board and the state school board agency.

Advice to Dr. Hana Jackson should include doing the right thing by allowing teachers to take on innovative leadership positions in trauma-informed care and not manipulating data. While data manipulation may seem like a solution, in the long run, honesty is the better policy.

*Case Study: Zero Means Zero*

Urban district; Mission, Vision, and Core Values 1b, c

Students with disabilities are less likely to receive disciplinary action than their non-disabled peers. That may mean that the manifestation determination meetings are finding that the students acted out as a result of their disabilities and receive different consequences. It may also suggest that teachers are less likely to write up students with disabilities for their infractions, and administrators less likely to assign consequences.

No students received corporal punishment. Either the administrators chose not to use this disciplinary action or Emerson City School District does not allow corporal punishment.

The superintendent may find grade-level data helpful. For example, it may be useful to see where the disparity in discipline begins and what trends occur. It may be useful to analyze the trends in SAT scores and in student attendance, and the numbers should be compared to the total enrollment.

The zero-tolerance policy has had an impact on discipline and academics at Emerson City School District. Changing the policy and providing the support teachers need would help to improve student performance. The superintendent should prepare her data for public presentations, gather feedback from stakeholders, and present the information to the school board. The superintendent should request that the policy be revoked.

Teachers, parents, students, administrators, representatives from the district police department, and community stakeholders should be part of the decision-making team. Overcoming the problem will require support and work from everyone.

*Case Study: A Personal Philosophy for the Public*

Suburban district; Mission, Vision, and Core Values 1f, g

Student achievement is a single performance measure at one point in time, much like an isolated snapshot. Student growth, on the other hand, measures progress between two points in the learning continuum. By analyzing data from student cohorts, educators can assess the effectiveness of the curriculum and instruction.

Because the math scores have shown little progress, Superintendent Ismail should meet with the campus administrators to pinpoint what the issue is. He'll also have to regain the trust of the teachers since he suggested on social media that they aren't doing their jobs.

Student performance is one of the first areas the superintendent will need to work on, but before that, he'll have to regain the trust and respect of the teachers. He will need to provide them with the support they need for student success.

Superintendent Ismail's opinion should be of concern to the board. His vision is not aligned with that of the district; it appears that his personal mission statement is nothing more than lip service. The board should change their rating.

Answers will vary regarding the personal mission statement, but it should align with district expectations.

## Case Study: White Flight

Suburban district; Mission, Vision and Core Values 1b, e

Depending on state law, superintendents may be able to prevent student transfers. Caution is advised in doing so because of the negative publicity it would generate about the district. In turn, this negativity could cause future residents to reconsider moving into the school district. A better course of action is to work closely with parents and students to meet their needs. Parents may transfer their children to another district if a school is designated as unsafe or does not meet acceptable standards.

The superintendent failed to monitor a variety of data elements and intervene. As the student demographics were changing, he should have adjusted the mission and vision statement to align with the needs of the students. Academics were in decline, and behavior problems increased. The behaviors were a sign that students were not being successful academically; they were acting out because they weren't learning in class.

Minority enrollment and grades have increased. The correlation between this information and the reduction in students taking advanced coursework suggests GPA averages increased due to having fewer students enrolled in rigorous courses.

The superintendent should meet with parents to better understand their concerns regarding the quality of education in the district. By including culturally diverse families in the discussion, the district may be able to help everyone find common ground: the education of children, regardless of their color, their background, or their prior knowledge.

While answers will vary, getting the community involved is the first priority. As students' needs change, so must the way the district responds change.

By obtaining community involvement, residents have a stake in what's happening. Then the district can respond to student need, continuing to provide remedial coursework to close learning gaps while still offering advanced courses for students. The district will need to provide teacher training in the areas of instruction and discipline.

## Case Study: Defining Moments

Urban district; Mission, Vision, and Core Values 1a

The students are the most critical components of the district. They appear to feel disenfranchised, and their parents are seeing some of that as well. The students are dissatisfied with extracurricular activities, so it may be an indication that the school district is not attuned to student interests. The involvement of the most complimentary groups and the community members at large and the school board in district operations may have cloaked their objectivity.

Answers about priorities may vary, but without school safety and good classroom management, student achievement won't improve. Even students interested in learning won't be able to get what they need because of the interruptions during class. The lack of school safety may also be affecting attendance for students and faculty.

A district will retain good teachers by giving them the support they need in the classroom and providing cutting-edge professional development. Teachers need a rigorous curriculum, books and materials, and the tools with which to teach. Reducing bureaucratic procedures can help teachers focus on instruction. Every teacher needs a personalized professional development plan.

To convince the school board to allow the superintendent, Dr. Serene Fielding, to make the necessary changes, she can show them the data she's collected and how the results are interconnected. It may be a good idea to show comparative data by showing the board how similar districts in the area are performing and what innovative strategies they use. Finally, the superintendent can encourage board members to speak with the members of the community.

## Chapter Two: Coming to Terms with Ethics in Our Profession

### Case Study: Changing the Schools to Prison Pipeline

Suburban district; Ethics and Professional Norms 2c, e; Equity and Cultural Responsiveness 3c; Meaningful Engagement of Families and Community 8b

Dr. Isra Styles should gather data from her own district to compare them to the national trends. She should, with a committee of educators, review especially the discipline and attendance data, breaking it down by ethnicity, gender, and other subpopulations. The analysis will point to changes that should be made, and the summary can be shared within the community for feedback and input.

Reducing the number of police officers and increasing the number of counselors would likely take place over the summer since most schools hire employees on a contractual basis. The change in staffing numbers isn't the only initiative to consider. The district should determine how best to provide continued support to students. Equity and diversity training, student advisory boards, and regular community meetings are ways of making this happen.

Dr. Isra Styles could ask a parent community for recommendations about the number of positions on a campus, but not specifically who should be hired for those positions. Parents could recommend that the counselors, for example, be representative of the population they serve, but they cannot select the person.

As for Dr. Isra Styles's own ethnicity, answers will vary. Her ethnicity shouldn't matter, but it may produce cultural bias.

## Case Study: What's in a Name?

Urban district; Ethics and Professional Norms 2d; Equity and Cultural Responsiveness 3a; Meaningful Engagement of Families and Community 8b

The sooner Dr. Brown meets with the community leaders for BLM, the better. Being responsive to concerns is one way to validate concerns and show that a group's opinions matter. Dr. Brown should prepare an agenda that allows for open remarks, explain the board policy regarding the naming of schools, and share the district's demographics by race and ethnicity. According to the numbers, Black students are predicted to make up 16 percent of the district's student population, not 50 percent. Renaming at least half the schools after national Black leaders would disenfranchise the other races and ethnicities.

However, the district predicts that it will see growth, and it will require new schools. There will be plenty of opportunities to name schools after community leaders in the future.

Race and ethnicity can matter in how the school board is constituted, especially if community members feel as though they have no representation and no voice. Dr. Brown could explain ways how communities could be more active and have a voice in schools, including setting up parent councils, attending school board meetings, and running for the school board.

The superintendent could disallow the protest and shirts on the grounds that maintaining order and safety is paramount in every school. Additionally, the Black population is the second smallest ethnicity in the district. However, students from other races and ethnicities may want to participate in expressing their First Amendment rights. The school district must take care that this expression does not result in unsafe behavior. If the students are allowed to protest on the behalf of BLM, then the district must allow other groups the same opportunity in the future.

Dr. Brown should also keep the school board informed of his meeting with the BLM community activists and its outcome.

*Case Study: Finances First*

Urban district; Operations and Management 9d, h; Ethics and Professional Norms 3f

While answers may vary, one of the biggest problems is paying bills in a timely manner. The district has money on hand, which would indicate that it is solvent. However, inaccuracy, carelessness, and a lack of urgency seem to permeate the district when it comes to fiscal responsibility.

To change the indifference seen across the district, Dr. Clifford will have to implement new finance practices. These could include department self-audits of paying purchase orders on time, monitoring the bills that are not paid within thirty and sixty days, and establishing procedures and deadlines for all finance activities. It is urgent that the superintendent determine the debt to cash reserve ratio.

Finally, the district must hire an independent accounting firm to audit every department, and the district must report the findings accurately to the public.

Closing the school district would mean liquidating assets and leaving buildings empty. Students and employees would have to go elsewhere, leaving the community in a financial predicament and placing a burden on neighboring districts.

To avoid this, Dr. Clifford should implement new policies and procures for fiscal accountability, and she should monitor them closely for compliance. If needed, the local education service centers and the state school board association can help put these together for her, and they will also provide any training that is necessary.

*Case Study: Every Child Matters*

Suburban district; Ethics and Professional Norms 2b, c

The reading, math, U.S. history, and geography scores are based on a scale of 0–500. The Friedman Public School's results in reading and math are higher than the national average, which may indicate phenomenal instruction, but could be a cause for concern because they jumped so significantly. The writing, science, and civics scores are based on a 0–300 scale. They too increased, but not as much.

The CBAs given throughout the year are more indicative of student learning than the national exam results are. The teachers used holistic scoring methods on student compositions, and the results suggest the instruction was better aligned with the curriculum and assessment.

The superintendent should conduct an investigation into the accusation of cheating on the national exam answer documents. She may need to remove Carly Birch from her position with pay until the matter is resolved. It is also advisable to confer with the district attorney. In addition, the superintendent will need to inform parents about the national scores, which cannot be used to gauge student performance, nor should they be used as a means to determine placement. The superintendent will also have to handle media requests. She will not be able to divulge details, but she will need to be as transparent and decisive as possible.

To assure testing integrity, no person should be alone with the tests. A requirement that at least one other person be present would prevent a single person from altering answer documents. The district needs to identify and implement rigorous requirements regarding assessment procedures, especially for packing and sending them out for scoring.

Hiring a friend is not considered nepotism, so it is permissible to hire a friend, but not recommended. The superintendent should not have hired her friend if she would be the friend's supervisor.

Paper answer documents can be altered or changed. They can be lost. They are, however, sometimes considered more student-friendly if test-takers do not have adequate computer skills. Computer-based assessments are easier to administer, and they are more secure. They can be a challenge to technology-poor districts.

## Case Study: Tomatoe, Tomato, What's Your Imago?

Suburban district; Ethics and Professional Norms 2d, e

Exeter Public Schools have the lowest scores in the area. Like the other districts, their mathematics scores are lower than their reading scores. Hispanic males score lower on standardized performances than other groups. Students in the bilingual/ELL program seem to perform poorly, as do students identified for special education services. Overall, females in Exeter outperform the males. There may be a correlation between the teachers' years of experience and the type of instruction being delivered. The teachers may be using outdated methodologies to teach the students.

Superintendents may need to vent about overall performance, but no one should allow a superintendent to blame lack of success on the students or to brag about threatening employees to do a better job or else.

The business of a superintendent is to advocate for the students and families in the district, which Superintendent Jenner was not willing to do. In addition to providing resources, funding, and inspiring a collegial work environment based on best practices in the profession, superintendents demonstrate social-emotional insight and understanding of all students' and staff members' backgrounds and cultures. They welcome diversity.

Although answers will vary, the superintendents at the meeting should have spoken up and echoed Superintendent Gilmore's sentiment: we are in the business of educating every child who enrolls, regardless of their background.

The area superintendents seem to have a history of collaborating with each other, as evidenced by Johnson and Gilmore. They may decide to reach out to Jenner, mentoring and guiding him in overcoming frustration.

## Chapter Three: Creating a Sense of Belonging, Inclusivity in a Post-Pandemic World

*Case Study: Low Income, High Expectations*

Suburban District; Equity and Cultural Responsiveness 3c; Meaningful Engagement of Families and Community 8b; School Improvement 10a

Dr. Muhammad Wooden should schedule meetings with the administration and the faculty at Tinkerton High School to gain a deeper understanding of the problem the teachers face on a day-to-day basis. He should also talk with families in the community to see what is important to them. For example, are the teenagers being asked to help support the family financially, and is there enough for teens to do outside of the school day and school year? What problems need to be solved?

Sending the students to other campuses in the district is not an option, because doing so will create overcrowding as well as transportation issues.

Instead, the superintendent must convince stakeholders that all students, regardless of their socioeconomic status, are entitled to a quality education that will prepare them for their futures. Low expectations for marginalized groups of students are never okay.

Dr. Muhammad Wooden may want to encourage the campus leaders to analyze additional data such as student and faculty attendance, program spending, and teacher retention/professional development. The district must provide appropriate training and mentorship to teachers needing it, and the district must commit to funding initiatives to the fullest extent possible so that the Tinkerton High School students can benefit from the district's resources.

Although action steps may vary from superintendent to superintendent, the district school leader should build a team of educators who can transform the campus and re-energize the students and their teachers. The leader must also commit sufficient resources to the effort and will need to be visible in the community they are trying to reach.

## Case Study: Preparing for Diversity

Rural district; Equity and Cultural Responsiveness 3a, b, c

The data have been presented for the most recent year. A longitudinal report would verify the evolution to a more diverse student population, but the district shouldn't spend too much time on the history. A better approach would be to look at additional data, such as state assessment scores, college and career readiness results, graduation rates, and so on.

Superintendent Dr. Dumas may also wish to review how much money in the past three years has been left unspent by campuses. This information may help him formulate a plan going forward.

The superintendent might not have noticed the funds being returned if the various departments at Central Office Administration pooled the resources and spent them with returning them to the state. He may have been less involved in meeting with and talking to the principals than he should have been.

To make sure the students in the district get the services to which they are entitled, each program director should complete a comprehensive review and share this information with campus leaders, board members, and the community. Reports should include suggestions for improving student services and academics for each ethnicity represented so no child is made to feel excluded or disenfranchised.

The superintendent should require cultural diversity and sensitivity training for the campus leaders, and this training should be replicated for the faculty at each campus as well. In addition, teachers will need professional development in reaching culturally diverse populations, and even the school libraries may need upgrades to include ethnically diverse literature.

Although answers will vary, Dr. Dumas could consider the following next steps: meet individually with the high school principal, provide diversity training, monitor the instructional and fiscal programs more closely, check in with leaders during the school year by reviewing fluid data, and engage in more community outreach—and encourage the campus leaders and faculty to do the same.

## Case Study: How We've Always Done It

Rural district; Mission, Vision, and Core Values 1c; Equity and Cultural Responsiveness 3a, b

Under federal law, a district is required to provide bilingual education to children only if there are twenty or more students in a grade level speaking the same native language at home. The level of bilingual instruction depends on the level of limited English proficiency. It is not cost-effective to offer bilingual instruction to two students in a school, but the school should monitor for increasing numbers of bilingual children and plan for their needs. In the meantime, however, the school must provide ESL services to all students needing it.

The gap in scores could depend on several factors, including the quality of instruction, whether teachers have been adequately trained in special population strategies, and how well the curriculum might be aligned. There is also a possibility that the teachers are not engaging students in the lessons; they are not culturally relevant.

The district offers a traditional list of extracurricular activities. At one time, these were the backbone of the community, representative of what mattered to the residents. The numbers of students enrolled represent a small portion of the student body. Most students are not in any extracurricular activity. Now that the Dwainville demographics have changed, the activities should too, by reflecting what interests the students the most.

Now that the AFL-CIO (American Federation of Labor and Congress of Industrial Organizations) is involved in the Dwainville situation, the superintendent should schedule a meeting in private with the representative and have the school attorney present while they discuss the points of contention. The superintendent (and the school board) will likely have to make concessions in several areas because they must provide a culturally appropriate education.

They should be prepared to discuss the influence of the Fellowship of Christian Athletes (a club with a membership of six), and whether the club should be allowed to continue meeting to pray before school. By allowing the club to remain active, the district must also allow for other religious clubs to assemble if they follow the same rules.

Had the superintendent and his school board been proactive when the demographics were changing, they could have embraced and encouraged the diversity.

*Case Study: Emotional and Behavioral Disorders (EBD) in Pine Tree*

Rural district; Equity and Cultural Responsiveness 3a, d; Community of Care and Support for Students 5e; School Improvement 10f

Garland Shepherd should appoint a committee of special education personnel, teachers, and campus administrators to look for data collection systems that will allow them to analyze behaviors and make informed decisions regarding trauma-informed care. Pine Tree must make an effort to mask the data and save it over time for analysis.

The increase of students identified with EBD will place additional demands on teachers and administrators. The superintendent could recommend one full-time equivalent (FTE) for every 600 students identified with EBD in the district. Persons in these positions could provide trauma-informed care professional development for teachers. They could model ways in which to work with EBD students. The district could use ESSA (Every Student Succeeds Act) and IDEA (Individuals with Disabilities Act) funds for the positions because a diagnosis of EBD requires *DSM-5* testing and identification as a special education student if the behavior interferes with access to instruction.

Should the district decide not to hire support personnel, then Shepherd would have to find other ways to train teachers and offer support in the classroom.

Shepherd should tell the community about this new initiative once the new positions are approved. Campus administrators can provide information sessions for parents.

## Case Study: Period Shaming

*Suburban district; Equity and Cultural Responsiveness 3a, d; Community of Care and Support for Students 5e*

Safety first, especially when it comes to crowd control. Superintendent Disdale should call campus security/911 to have the fighting parents removed. They are disrupting a school event, and their fighting creates a dangerous situation. Until first responders arrive, ask people to move away from the fighting, but do not personally separate them.

Menstrual bullying, also known as period shaming, affects 25 percent of girls in middle school, and eight out of ten have missed class due to lack of access to feminine hygiene products. Girls who live in poverty have had to use substitutions like leaves, socks, and folded sheets of notebook paper to stave the bleeding associated with their menstrual cycles (Milianta-Laffin (2022; Pahr 2019).

Even if she truly felt overwhelmed by having to provide "one more thing" for students, Mrs. De Leon's response has no place in schools today. When basic student needs are taken care of by the management (think Maslow), the students can concentrate on other things like academics. Clearly, Mrs. De Leon had not addressed the root cause of bullying, which has placed her school in this perilous predicament. By overlooking her personal opinion, Mrs. De Leon could (and should have) provided for her students. Superintendent Disdale would be right to consider the nonrenewal of the principal's contract because she did not address attendance, discipline, or academics in an effective manner—nor did she ensure that each student is treated fairly, respectfully, and with an understanding of each student's culture and context.

Placing a menstruation station discreetly in each school could assure girls that they would have the supplies necessary for that time of the month. By addressing the problem openly and head-on, the school would eliminate period shaming. Attendance and scores would improve.

Schools could partner with local businesses to provide pads, wipes, and so on. Parent groups could hold fundraisers as well. An essential step toward having menstruation stations in schools is education—teaching parents what to expect, especially if they are from different cultures and religions. For example, schools could reassure parents concerned about tampon use and virginity that the school will provide only pads.

Answers will vary, but the girls in today's school hope you'll say yes—and then make it happen.

## Chapter Four: Creating Communities to Champion All Students

### Case Study: Navigating Chartered Waters

Urban district; Community of Care and Support for Students 5c; Operations and Management 9d

The per pupil expenditures from campus to campus likely vary because of the special programs in place at each location. For example, the ELL students at Jefferson High School receive some additional federal funds, as do the special education students at Smith High School.

To develop a formula for equity in student funding, the superintendent could recommend a per pupil amount based on the district average generated through taxes. Additional funding would also be determined on a per pupil basis, such as whether or not a student might be served by Title II or IDEA funds.

No child should be denied what he or she needs to be as academically successful as his or her peers. One of the subsequent areas to explore and correct is performance in meeting accountability standards.

The superintendent could also review teacher retention data and community satisfaction surveys to develop a clearer understanding of the community's perception of the schools.

The superintendent, Dr. Layann Hackner, could then explain her decisions and the rationale for them by showing the formulas that she and her leadership team developed.

### Case Study: Getting Them All across the Stage

Urban district; Curriculum, Instruction, and Assessment 4a; Community of Care and Support for Students 5e

The cohort graduation rates at Creek City High School are lower than the district, city, and state results. The leadership team should look closely at the schools' expectations for their students and then gather a variety of data for analysis.

This data should include academic performance, student engagement, attendance, college/career readiness measurements, staffing experience and retention, and program funding. Next, the team should consider external factors such as the socioeconomic status of families in the community. Do students need to work to help support their families? What are the crime rates in the area?

The intervention team for Creek City High School should include administration, teachers, assistants, families, and especially students. The superintendent should also include transportation and student services in the discussion.

An incoming superintendent may decide to keep Mr. Foster on staff until contract renewals in the spring. At that time, she or he may non-renew the contract if there is no evidence of significant improvement in the graduation rates among each cohort at Creek City High School. The superintendent may move Mr. Foster out of curriculum and instruction and into another role until contract renewals as long as there is no change in pay. The same would be true for the principal of Creek City High School.

Mr. Foster should not apply for the position unless he has a plan that will be effective in raising the graduation rates at Creek City High School.

## Case Study: To V or Not to V

Urban district; Curriculum, Instruction, and Assessment 4d, e

Dr. Fatimah Williams and her cabinet should look for variables between the studies and how they are delivering instruction. Virtual replacement instruction is highly effective when used by itself. If the district requires teachers to teach face-to-face and virtually at the same time, the effectiveness of instruction may be compromised.

Dr. Fatimah Williams should look at a variety of data, including grades and behavior reports. All of the data should be broken down by subpopulation to check for possible disparity and inequality between gender, race, ethnicity, and more.

There are several options available for providing virtual instruction, including setting aside a specific amount of time for it or having in-class and virtual teaching roles. Teachers who must quarantine at home may be able to teach virtually or substitute for absent teachers. The district may consider "curriculum in a box" models for virtual students. All virtual students, however, should have to meet district protocols for attendance and grades or risk losing the privilege or learning virtually form home or another location.

Dr. Fatimah Williams should meet first with staff and see what they need to be successful with the extended delivery system. Then the interim superintendent should meet with the community school to explain the decision and how instruction will be handled. She can also answer any questions parents might have.

Although answers may vary, many incoming superintendents will hope that the staff will feel as though they have had the training, they need to be effective teachers who have been able to address the academic, behavioral, emotional, and social needs of their students.

*Case Study: Back to School*

Suburban district; Ethics and Professional Norms 2c; Community of Care and Support for Students 5a; Professional Capacity of School Personnel 6h

The priority when resuming instruction in the school setting is safety. Students, their families, and the staff must know that they will be taken care of. With that in mind, any protocols set forth must take these concerns—and the data—into consideration. For example, since the virus is spread more easily through aerosols, the district may consider suspending music and choir classes. The district may also wish to establish cleaning and disinfecting protocols that focus more areas identified in current research. Other protocols should include safe practices, like hand washing and mask wearing.

Communication with staff and the community should be transparent. Students can be included in age-appropriate conversions that do not cause panic. Teachers can instruct their students about the potential for positive COVID-19 spread. The superintendent must be clear that every decision is made with people and their safety first. However, the district is also in the business of instruction, and instruction must continue. Campuses have to meet the academic and social needs of their students. This may be done with creative scheduling that alternates time in school with virtual instruction—a blended approach.

Discussions about COVID-19 precautions present educators with a unique opportunity. For several decades, education has lamented that it needs disruption. The disruption is here, in the form of a virus, and superintendent Tagreed Jaramillo could use this opportunity to redefine what instruction could look like in the twenty-first century.

The district should send parents regular updates regarding positive cases in schools and any of the precautions being taken.

*Case Study: Separate but Equal*

Rural district; Community of care and support for students 5b, c

Because the numbers for credit recovery are the highest in the 10th grade, the superintendent should look into the instruction in 8th and 9th grades. There may be a curriculum alignment issue, or a problem with instructional delivery. By talking to students, parents, and the teachers, the superintendent might be able to formulate a clear picture of what's happening.

The number of students needing credit recovery in the 12th grade might be lower because teens are dropping out of school rather than catching up on credits. More data are required.

Superintendent Miller should contact the district attorney before taking the matter into his own hands. It appears that the at-risk students were sent to a campus known for exacerbating health conditions. This isn't the first time the campus has had problems with mold and mildew. However, prior to its repurposing, the Fordyce housed the intermediate students—all of them.

Whether or not the district is liable for the health of the teachers may depend on the state in which they live. Generally speaking, the courts have upheld that a teacher cannot sue a school district for having mold in the school building.

The district might be able to salvage the Fordyce Campus by removing the walls and insulation, cleaning what's left, and rebuilding the campus, but the effort will be costly.

## Chapter Five: Cultivating Meaningful Professional Engagement for the Communities We Lead

*Case Study: But They Have a Long Runway*

Urban district; Professional Capacity of School Personnel 5a, c, d

The low scores may be the result of several issues, including a poorly aligned curriculum, students instructing themselves, and a faculty that has not been equipped with the teaching strategies they need.

The professional development is intense at the beginning of the school year, and it immerses the teachers in the work ahead. However, the training stops there. The best research-based professional development occurs over time. Teachers cannot be expected to learn everything at once and be prepared for the academic year ahead. Adult learners have an ongoing need for collaborative learning experiences, and their professional development should reflect that.

By working collaboratively with the state monitors, Superintendent Khadijeh Julius may be able to find a way to adapt her educational program to better meet the needs of the students and still achieve the school's mission statement. By bringing the parents (and teachers) into the discussion, she could develop a comprehensive plan that would instill ownership and responsibility.

A variety of changes could be made at Namaste Charter School. Two of the most significant changes might be creating a structured day for students and providing ongoing professional development for the teachers. This plan should allow for instruction, networking, and coaching/mentoring.

The state should close low-performing charter schools much sooner than they are considering for Namaste Charter School. By delaying the inevitable, the student enrolled here are losing years of schooling that will have to be made up elsewhere, likely at a considerable investment of time and money.

*Case Study: Sure Shots*

Suburban district; Professional Capacity of School Personnel 5g

A superintendent may want to look at a deeper data analysis of discipline and school safety by looking at the subpopulations creating the data. For example, knowing the race and ethnicity may reveal if there is a tendency to over-react or over-report unsafe situations. It also may be helpful to pinpoint if one community in Centerton is experiencing more dangerous behavior than another because the students may be bringing the challenges to school with them.

Opinions will vary regarding allowing school employees to carry weapons on campus. Answers should be thoughtful and take into consideration some of the following:

- Whether insurance premiums for the district will rise or the insurance companies will no longer insure the district.
- What type of campuses are in the district? Alternative campuses and secure facilities would likely not have weapons on campus.
- Whether the district will purchase weapons or allow employees to carry their own.
- The likelihood of having to pay for range practice time and ammo so employees can maintain their shooting proficiency.
- What will the district do if the weapon is lost/stolen/misplaced?

The pepper spray incident is a workplace injury, and workman's compensation will cover the doctor visits. Expect the premiums for worker's comp to rise.

Superintendent Valerie Alexandria should meet with the middle school principal, Ben Garza, personally to explain that although he was a star pupil at the firearms training, he failed his psychological test and will not be able to carry on campus. She should tell him that the results of his evaluation are strictly confidential and have no bearing on his performance evaluation. Mr. Garza is likely protected under the Americans with Disabilities Act, Section 504, and cannot be discriminated against.

## Case Study: Evaluation Devaluation

Suburban School District; Professional Community for Teachers and Staff 7d, g; Professional Capacity of School Personnel 6a, e

The job of monitoring the campus principals usually falls to the assistant superintendent for curriculum and instruction, or to the superintendent himself. The assistant superintendent or directors for curriculum and instruction, finance, and human resources are the ones you gather information to give to the superintendent if the superintendent evaluates the job performance of the principals. In this situation the human resources director or assistant superintendent should have monitored compliance with deadlines and requirements.

By asking an employee what here she would like to see happen as a consequence, You involve the employee thinking critically rather than emotionally about the situation. Often, the employee will come up with something fair and equitable and will often accept the consequence because he or she had some sort of input.

Although the superintendent could approve the transfer request or overturn the evaluations and contract decisions, it would be wise to let the human resources intervene, sending non-partial observers to the campus to conduct the formal observations. In the meantime, the superintendent can have a serious talk with the elementary campus principal about following the protocol and making sure that teachers have the support they need earlier in the school year.

In most states, state assessment results cannot be considered part of the teachers' evaluation. In California, for example, The Stull Act has been in effect since 1971, and this piece of legislature prohibits administrators from using ever-changing assessment protocols in teacher evaluation of instruction.

The elementary principal was in the wrong regarding teacher evaluations because she did not follow the protocol set forth by the district. If the teacher's union contacted the superintendent regarding these evaluations at the principal's actions, superintendent shouldn't tell the union that the matter is being investigated and the district expectations is that all employees regardless of their position in the district follow the protocol set forth for fair and impartial annual evaluations of teacher performance.

## Case Study: More than Money

Rural district; Meaningful Engagement of Families and Community 8h, i

The National Center for Education Data found that, on average, local and state governments each account for 45 percent of the overall education budget in a school district. Funds from the federal government account for approximately 10 percent of the budget. The local and state funding budget cuts are some of the smallest, and the federal cuts, although larger, would affect only

10 percent of the budget. The district can expect cuts, but they are unlikely to be as painful as the superintendent is predicting.

Dr. Bentley understands the significance of bringing together people of diverse backgrounds because she serves on a committee herself. By assembling stakeholders before the board meeting, she could have offered her suggestions, but more importantly, gather input from everyone else, including administrators, teachers, parents, and community members.

If the district is not already doing so, it could become a co-op member to take advantage of lower prices when purchasing supplies, fuel, and even benefits programs for employees. Other ways to generate income could be through bonds and grants. The district may want to adopt a university model of commerce; some colleges are selling what their students produce. For example, agricultural departments are selling plants, vegetables, and flowers in farmers' markets, and business departments sell accounting services. The money generated goes back to student programs.

If the district is unable to offset costs, it will have to make budget cuts. Because rural districts are often less efficient with their money than urban districts, the superintendent should ask for an efficiency review. Any services that are duplicated and can be produced for less should be explored. If the district must make cuts, it must do so with the greatest amount of transparency possible, and Dr. Bentley should involve stakeholders at all levels.

## Case Study: Bonding with the Community

Suburban district; Meaningful Engagement of Families and Community 8g, h

Keeping the community informed about district business, especially progress regarding the bonds in place is always a good idea. The caveat is that the information must be updated so the community responsible for these bonds are in the know. Having a single resource for everything about the bonds promotes communication.

Bonds are cheap money. By having a bond, a district is often able to purchase big ticket items like land and buildings with far less cost than traditional loans. Borrowing money is often the only way for schools to prepare for future growth because they simply do not have the cash reserves on hand, and they cannot use their maintenance and operations funds for construction.

Some of the proposed expenses in the third bond package are questionable. For example, a new vehicle for the superintendent sounds more like a luxury item than a necessity. Security camera and handheld technology will be outdated well before the bond is paid in full. Purchasing these items on credit isn't much different than buying breakfast tacos with your credit card at a service station and then taking twenty years or more to pay them off, because you can.

Conventional wisdom has always maintained that municipal bonds are low-risk investments. They haven't needed insurance because there has been little chance of default. However, public organizations like those in cities (i.e., Detroit) have defaulted on municipal bonds in the past few years, so there may be a trend toward adding insurance into bond packages.

To garner support for the proposed bond, the superintendent must talk to as many people as he can about the issue. Speaking at school events is not enough. He should also speak to civic and social groups like Lions and Rotary. Political organizations and church groups also make good venues for getting out the word.

## Chapter Six: Supporting Sustainable School Improvement

### Case Study: Be My Guest

Rural district; Operations and Management 9d

Because Mrs. Brown is the curriculum director, she has a responsibility to make sure that any textbook adoption is aligned to the subject standards. One of the first things she should have told the teachers is that any adoption must be in alignment with their needs and the required standards. Summit is the least aligned to district needs.

The superintendent can ask for the voting results. When the truth comes out, the superintendent should be prepared to listen to the curriculum director's rationale for her choice.

Expressing disappointment and concern about the low reading and writing scores is appropriate for a superintendent. However, the person in this position should take care that their statements are not threatening.

When Mrs. White finds out about the vacation for Mrs. Brown and her children, she will have to take action, possibly releasing Mrs. Brown from her contract immediately. District employees cannot accept gifts from vendors. In addition, Mrs. White may have violated this law because of the many lunches she had with Ben Smiley from ABC.

While answers may vary about the best textbook for the adoption, Acme comes closest in meeting the district's requirements. Although it's not the cheapest adoption, it is not the most expensive, either. Best of all, it is most closely aligned to the standards for reading and writing.

### Case Study: Continuous Improvement Begins Here

Suburban district; School Improvement 10c, d

Superintendent Mahmoud Gilmore should speak to the campus administrators in general terms at first, commending them for growth in reading. He can point out how they did in comparison to other districts, and he should especially mention the growth over the past three years.

Mathematics, on the other hand, seems to be an issue not just for Ballantine schools but also for many districts in the area. The superintendent should ask the administrators to explore both the reasons for the growth and decline in scores. For example, White students seem to be outperforming their peers. It would be wise to look into the reasons for this:

- Over-representation in gifted classes?
- A general bias on the part of the teachers?
- Curriculum that is one-sided and culturally biased?

The team ought to look at each subpopulation because some groups are outperforming others. It would also be helpful for each school to have a breakdown or the passing rate by grade level and performance on each learning standard.

It is important to note that the subpopulations are performing similarly to the average overall scores. As a rule of thumb, reading scores are up across the board. Mathematics scores are down. This would suggest the problem with the instruction or alignment in mathematics, not with a specific subpopulation.

The district ought to check in with the Churchton and Dandelion districts to see what they are doing to improve student achievement. Send a team of teachers to visit the teachers in those two districts.

It's best to confront the principal who speaks out against a colleague. His remark came across as bullying, and it should not be tolerated. Rather than allow for the bullying, the superintendent should insist on the campuses working together. That's why he put them in these groups. Avoid singling out the principal who did the harassing; speak with her in private about the matter.

It may be effective for the teachers to see the average scores for each district in the area, but they need data that drill down into each subject. They should find out how their students performed overall, and they also need to know how well students did on the learning objectives. In addition, they should look at not only how many students answered the question correctly but which students selected which incorrect answer.

It was important to bring the community into the discussion about the reading program when it was adopted. The district will need to do the same with a math initiative. The sooner parents know about the initiative, the quicker they can get behind it and support it. The superintendent can remind them that a new approach worked for reading; it should also work for mathematics.

## Case Study: Reading between the Lines

Suburban district; School Improvement 10e

Comparing performance at each grade level across districts, educators can determine if there is a systemic issue or if it is more isolated.

The schools in the Ballentine district should dig deeper with their data to see where the difficulty lies. Until they analyze how students answered questions, compare the questions to the curriculum for alignment, and look at the best instructional practices, they won't be able to see where the challenge is.

The district may need to purchase a new math program if the current one is not aligned, and it may still need to provide additional training for their teachers, considering how little teaching experience they have.

By isolating the skills and concepts students need for each grade level, the Ballentine district can determine how to implement their initiative. The initiative should include 3rd-/4th-grade teachers and 6th-/7th-grade teachers since they will be working together and likely following their students next year.

Rather than have the superintendent recommend the specific strategies, the teachers must identify what they need. They are the ones in the classroom, closest to the students. The strategies they select will be more likely to be implemented. The superintendent's job is to help provide resources, not come up with and execute the plan.

He or she should make it clear, however, that growth will be closely monitored. The district cannot wait until the end of the year to see if their strategies have worked. If they are not working, the district will have to change its strategy to one that works.

## Case Study: What's in a Grade?

Rural district; School Improvement 10d, e

Grades can be subjective, especially when including participation. Unless there is an alignment between learning standards and the grading practice, the grade will not reflect learning.

Participation and organizational skills are an implicit part of learning standards. If they are included as part of a grade, they should not constitute half of the evaluation each six weeks. Grades must accurately and honestly reflect student learning.

The superintendent must revise the mission statement to something that focuses more on achievement and performance. She will need to make sure all stakeholders understand the new mission statement and not take it out of context. The grading policy will also need to change. It's appropriate to require re-teach and deadlines for turning in revised assignments. Parents need advance notice of all changes once approved by the school board. The district must develop a plan for identifying students requiring academic intervention during the school year and the summer.

In the future, the district should measure student success through student performance and student growth. Student growth will reveal whether the new strategies regarding instruction and grading are effective.

The superintendent should tell parents that the district leaders and teachers are going to focus on bringing curriculum, instruction, and assessment into better alignment so that when students receive a grade, it's an authentic measure of progress. The changes won't happen overnight, but they will make a difference.

## Case Study: Social Media Threat

Urban district; School Improvement 10h, i

Districts can set policy regarding social media engagement, but in doing so, the school district must be prepared to monitor posts and follow up with consequences for misuse or violations.

A hotly debated topic, social media monitoring is not always an effective method of monitoring student and employee activity. Some people advocate for mining social media in order to prevent violent acts. Others decry it as a violation of privacy—especially of minors.

It may be helpful to know the time of day during which posts of concern were made. The current data can only be used to steer future training and intervention. For example, the significant increase in references to suicide suggest that suicide intervention training is necessary.

The superintendent, Dr. Aymen Lane, should contact the parents to express condolences. She should prioritize her intervention steps to reduce the likelihood of further harm.

The teachers were not supposed to have friended the student. Mrs. Dakota at least responded with concern and a phone number, but she should have reached out to authorities or the parents, if possible. Saying nothing makes Mr. Caroline complicit in the suicide because teachers are required to report suicidal ideations.

Suicidal ideations and intent to create violence are among the first areas in which to intervene because of the likelihood for harm and loss of life. Once these emergencies have been addressed, the school district should address cyberbullying, because if left unchecked, it could lead to physical harm and even death.

# References

AASA. 2019. "Aspiring Superintendents Academy® for Educational Leaders: Hybrid Learning Model." https://www.aasa.org/aspiring-academy-blended.aspx

Akbulut, M. S., and J. R. Hill. 2020. "Case-based Pedagogy for Teacher Education: An Instructional Model." *Contemporary Educational Technology* 12 (2). https://files.eric.ed.gov/fulltext/EJ1274346.pdf

Ameta, D., S. Tiwari, and P. Singh. 2020. "A Preliminary Study on Case-based Learning Teaching Pedagogy: Scope in SE Education." In *Proceedings of the 13th Innovations in Software Engineering Conference on Formerly Known as India Software Engineering Conference*, 1–12. February. http://seabed.in/upload/ISEC_2020___CBL__Preliminary_Review_Study_.pdf

Antonucci, J. J. 2012. "The Experience of School Superintendent Leadership in the 21st Century: A Phenomenological Study." Diss., Northeastern University. https://repository.library.northeastern.edu/files/neu:1154/fulltext.pdf

Bernhardt, V. L. 1999. *The school portfolio: A comprehensive framework for school improvement. (2nd ed.)*. Larchmont, NY: Eye on Education.

Bernhardt, V. 2004. *Data analysis for continuous school improvement (2nd. ed.)*. Larchmont, NY: Eye on Education.

Bonney, K. M. 2015. "Case Study Teaching Method Improves Student Performance and Perceptions of Learning Gains." *Journal of Microbiology & Biology Education* 16 (1): 21–28. https://doi.org/10.1128/jmbe.v16i1.846

Boston University Center for Teaching & Learning. n.d. "Using Case Studies to Teach." https://www.bu.edu/ctl/teaching-resources/using-case-studies-to-teach/

Çakmak, Z., and I. Hakan Akgün. 2018. "A Theoretical Perspective on the Case Study Method." *Journal of Education and Learning* 7 (1). https://files.eric.ed.gov/fulltext/EJ1157921.pdf

Cambron-McCabe, N., & McCarthy, M. 2005. Educating school leaders for social justice. *Educational Policy* 19(1), 201–222.

Cash, C., J. Brinkmann, and T. Price. 2022. *Superintendents' Leadership during the Pandemic. COVID-19 and the Classroom: How Schools Navigated the Great*

*Disruption*. The Rowman & Littlefield Publishing Group. ISBN 9781793651433. https://books.google.com/books?hl=en&lr=&id=xDZYEAAAQBAJ&oi=fnd&pg=PA123&dq=school+superintendents&ots=03dowkG5wL&sig=8pCT1t0AVPzSC-m3iBRlncVAnCo

Chenoweth, Karin. 2021. *Districts That Succeed Breaking the Correlation Between Race, Poverty, and Achievement*. Cambridge: Harvard Education Press.

Christensen, R. 1981. *Teaching by the Case Method*. Cambridge: Harvard Business School Press.

Danahy, A. 2022. "Add School Superintendents to the List of Jobs People Are Leaving in Pennsylvania and Nationally [Radio]." *All Things Considers, WESA*, February 3. https://www.wesa.fm/education/2022-02-03/add-school-superintendents-to-the-list-of-jobs-people-are-leaving-in-pennsylvania-and-nationally

Davis, B. W., and A. J. Bowers. 2019. Examining the career pathways of educators with superintendent certification. *Educational Administration Quarterly* 55 (1): 3–41. https://journals.sagepub.com/doi/pdf/10.1177/0013161X18785872

Diamantes, T., and J. Ovington. 2003. "Storytelling: Using a Case Method Approach in Administrator Preparation Programs." *Educational Leadership* 123 (3): 465–69. https://www.thefreelibrary.com/Storytelling%3A+using+a+case+method+approach+in+administrator . . . -a0100806935

DuFour, Richard. 2007. Professional Learning Communities: A Bandwagon, an Idea Worth Considering, or Our Best Hope for High Levels of Learning? *Middle School Journal (J1)* 39 (1), 4–8. https://eric.ed.gov/?id=EJ775771

Fullan, M. 2005. *Leading in a culture of change*. San Francisco, CA: Jossey-Bass.

Gamson, D. A. 2004. The infusion of corporate values into progressive education. *Journal of Educational Administration* 42 (2), 137–159.

Hart, W. H. 2018. "Is It Rational or Intuitive? Factors and Processes Affecting School Superintendents' Decisions When Facing Professional Dilemmas." *Educational Leadership Administration: Teaching and Program Development* 29 (1). https://files.eric.ed.gov/fulltext/EJ1172228.pdf

Hill, A. 2016. "A Case Study in a Superintendent's Leadership under Duress." Thesis, Northern Michigan University. https://commons.nmu.edu/cgi/viewcontent.cgi?article=1112&context=theses

Hoffer, E. R. 2020. "Case-based Teaching: Using Stories for Engagement and Inclusion." *International Journal on Social and Education Sciences* 2 (2): 75–80. https://files.eric.ed.gov/fulltext/EJ1263931.pdf

Hozien, W. 2019. *Superintendent Case Studies: Creating Meaningful Engagement*. Alexandria, VA: School Superintendents Association Publishers.

Jacobs, K., & Kritsonis, W. 2007. *An analysis of the objective ethics in educational leadership through Ayn Rand's The Virtue of Selfishness (1964)*. https://files.eric.ed.gov/fulltext/ED495311.pdf

Kowalski, T. 2011. *Case Studies on Educational Administration (Allyn & Bacon Educational Leadership)*. 6th ed. New York: Pearson. ISBN: 0137071302

Lawrence, S. E. 2008. "An Analysis of Various University-based Superintendent Preparation Programs and Their Alignment with Research Findings, Scholars' Opinions, and Practitioners' Experience." Diss., The University of Texas at Austin. https://repositories.lib.utexas.edu/bitstream/handle/2152/3937/lawrencesrs88288.pdf?sequence=2&isAllowed=y

Lynch, M. 2019. "How Do I become a School Superintendent?" *The Edvocate*, June 18. https://www.theedadvocate.org/how-do-i-become-a-school-superintendent/

Marx, G. 2006. *Future-focused leadership: preparing schools, students, and communities for tomorrow's realities*. Alexandria, VA: Association for Supervision and Curriculum Development.

Milianta-Laffin, Sarah. 2022. *How to Build a Menstruation Station at Your School*. Student Wellness, Edutopia. https://www.edutopia.org/article/how-build-menstruation-station-your-school?utm_content=linkpos1&utm_source=edu-newsletter&utm_medium=email&utm_campaign=weekly-2022-03-23

Miller, M. T., M. Y. Lu, and G. D. Gearhart. 2020. "From the Chalkboard to the Bank: Teaching Educational Leaders to Be Effective Fundraisers. Educational Leadership and Administration." *Teaching and Program Development* 32: 15. https://scholarworks.sjsu.edu/cgi/viewcontent.cgi?article=1011&context=edulead_pub

Nath, J. L. 2005. "The Roles of Case Studies in the Educational Field." *International Journal of Case Method Research & Application* 17: 3. http://www.wacra.org/PublicDomain/IJCRA%20xvii_iii%20Nath.pdf

National Policy Board for Educational Administration. 2015. *Professional Standards for Educational Leaders 2015*. Reston, VA: National Policy Board for Educational Administration. https://www.npbea.org/wp-content/uploads/2017/06/Professional-Standards-for-Educational-Leaders_2015.pdf

Noppe, R., Sheng, B., Webb, C., & Yager, S. 2013. Decision-making and problempractices of superintendents confronted by district dilemmas. *NCPEA International Journal of Educational Leadership Preparation* 8 (1), 103–120. https://www.ncpeapublications.org/attachments/article/532/Noppe.pdf

Pahr, Kristi. 2019. "Period Shaming: A Not-So New Type of Bullying Parents Need to Know about." *Parents Magazine*. https://www.parents.com/kids/problems/bullying/period-shaming-is-a-kind-of-bullying-parents-need-to-be-aware-of/

Perrone, F., and P. D. Tucker. 2019. "Shifting Profile of Leadership Preparation Programs in the 21st Century." *Educational Administration Quarterly* 55 (2): 253–95. https://doi.org/10.1177/0013161X18799473

Radi Afsouran, N., M. Charkhabi, S. A. Siadat, H. R. Oreyzi, R. Hoveida, and G. C. Thornton III. 2018. "Case-method Teaching: Advantages and Disadvantages in Organizational Training." *Journal of Management Development*. https://doi.org/10.1108/JMD-10-2017-0324

Rhodes, A., A. Wilson, and T. Rozell. 2020. "Value of Case-based Learning within STEM Courses: Is It the Method or Is It the Student?" *CBE—Life Sciences Education* 19 (3). https://www.lifescied.org/doi/pdf/10.1187/cbe.19-10-0200

Sampson, P. M., B. J. Alford, and R. L. Marshall. 2018. "Preparing Aspiring Superintendents to Lead School Improvement: Perceptions of Graduates for Program Development." *School Leadership Review* 5 (2). https://scholarworks.sfasu.edu/slr/vol5/iss2/3

Sapeni, M. A. A. R., and S. Said. 2020. "The Effectiveness of Case-based Learning in Increasing Critical Thinking of Nursing Students: A Literature Review." *Enfermeria Clinica* 30: 182–185. https://www.sciencedirect.com/science/article/abs/pii/S1130862119304243

Schiano, B., and E. Andersen. 2017. *Teaching with Cases Online*. Harvard Business Publishing. https://s3.amazonaws.com/he-product-images/docs/Article_Teaching_With_Cases_Online.pdf

Schumacher, J. A. 2013. "Case Based Learning: Preparing Adult Learners to become Thoughtful Leaders." *Conference Proceedings*. https://research.phoenix.edu/sites/default/files/user-presentation/Schumacher%20Case%20Based%20Learning%20Clute%20Institute%201314_1.pdf

Schweitzer, Karen, 2014. *How to write case study analysis?* Harvard Business Review. http://businessmajors.about.com/od/casestudies/ht/HowToCaseStudy.htm

Shields, C. M., & Edwards, M. M. 2005. *Dialogue is not just talk: A new ground for educational leadership*. New York: Peter Lang.

Summers, R. A. 2015. "The Superintendent as Transformational Leader: A Case Study Analysis of the Strategies, Initiatives and Processes Used by Superintendents of Exemplar 21st Century School Districts to Implement District-wide Change for the 21st Century." Diss., Brandman University. https://digitalcommons.umassglobal.edu/cgi/viewcontent.cgi?article=1056&context=edd_dissertations

Starratt, R. J. 1991. Building an Ethical School: A Theory for Practice in Educational Leadership. *Educational Administration Quarterly* 27 (2), 185–202. https://doi.org/10.1177/0013161X91027002005

Starratt, R. J. 2017. Leading Learning/Learning Leading: A retrospective on a life's work. *The selected works of Robert J. Starratt*. London: Routledge.

Sykes, G., and T. Bird. 1992. "Teacher Education and the Case Idea." *Review of Research in Education* 18: 457–521. https://doi.org/10.2307/1167305

Thiede, R. 2020. "Redesign and Development of the Superintendent Licensure Preparation Program for the 21st Century." *School Leadership Review* 15 (1). https://scholarworks.sfasu.edu/slr/vol15/iss1/25

Topperzer, M. K., L. I. Roug, L. Andrés-Jensen, P. Pontoppidan, M. Hoffmann, H. B. Larsen, . . . J. L. Sørensen. 2021. "Twelve Tips for Postgraduate Interprofessional Case-based Learning." *Medical Teacher*, 1–14. https://www.tandfonline.com/doi/pdf/10.1080/0142159X.2021.1896691

Wang, E. et al. 2018. "Launching a Redesign of University Principal Preparation Programs: Partners Collaborate for Change." Santa Monica, CA: RAND Education. https://www.wallacefoundation.org/knowledge-center/Documents/Launching-a-Redesign-of-University-Principal-Preparation-Programs.pdf

White, R. S. 2021. "What's in a First Name? America's K-12 Public School District Superintendent Gender Gap." *Leadership and Policy in Schools*, 1–17. https://www.tandfonline.com/doi/abs/10.1080/15700763.2021.1965169

Yale Poorvu Center for Teaching and Learning. 2021. "Case-based Learning." https://poorvucenter.yale.edu/strategic-resources-digital-publications/strategies-teaching/case-based-learning

Yavuz, O., P. Madonia, and V. M. Abolafia. 2018. "School Leadership Training: Are We Preparing Future Talent Managers?" *Uluslararası Liderlik Eğitimi Dergisi* 2 (2): 94–115. https://dergipark.org.tr/tr/download/article-file/486626

Zippia. 2021. "Superintendent Statistics and Facts in the U.S." https://www.zippia.com/superintendent-jobs/demographics/

# Bibliography

Behavioral Disorders. 2022. *Nsta.org.* https://www.nsta.org/behavioral-disorders.

Beusekom, M. 2020. *Yet More Data Support COVID-19 Aerosol Transmission.* CIDRAP. https://www.cidrap.umn.edu/news-perspective/2020/08/yet-more-data-support-covid-19-aerosol-transmission.

Brennan, K. 2018. "Data Show Cases of Anti-Muslim Bullying in Schools on the Rise." *The Philadelphia Inquirer.* http://www2.philly.com/philly/news/anti-muslim-bullying-schools-increase-lawsuit-st-dominics-20180722.html.

Burks, A. 2017. "White Parents Avoiding Failing Public Schools Isn't Segregation." *Medium.* https://medium.com/@ArnoldBurks/white-parents-avoiding-failing-black-schools-isnt-segregation-by-a-burks-cd941fa70e8c.

Chipp, T. 2017. "UPDATE: Texas Teacher Evaluation Lawsuit Settled." *Reporternews.com.* https://www.reporternews.com/story/news/education/2017/05/03/texas-teacher-evaluation-lawsuit-settled/101267090/.

*Cops and No Counselors- How the Lack of School Mental Health Staff Is Harming Students.* 2022. American Civil Liberties Union. https://www.aclu.org/issues/juvenile-justice/school-prison-pipeline/cops-and-no-counselors.

COVID-19 in PK-12 Public and Private Schools | Connecticut Data. 2022. *Data.ct.gov.* https://data.ct.gov/stories/s/mpdc-p8wg.

Disproportionality of Minority Students Identified with an Emotional/Behavioral Disorder. 2022. *Ufdc.ufl.edu.* https://ufdc.ufl.edu/UFE0041898/00001/12j.

Fensterwald, J. 2015. "Students Matter Sues Districts over Teacher Evaluations." *EdSource.* https://edsource.org/2015/students-matter-sues-districts-over-teacher-evaluations/83103.

Goldstein, D. 2016. "What Do White Parents Want in Schools? A Lot of White Kids." *Slate Magazine.* https://slate.com/human-interest/2016/07/when-white-parents-have-a-choice-they-choose-segregated-schools.html.

Gorman, L. 2003. "School Spending Raises Property Values." *NBER.* https://www.nber.org/digest/jan03/school-spending-raises-property-values.

Herold, B. 2017. "The Case(s) Against Personalized Learning." *Education Week*. https://www.edweek.org/technology/the-cases-against-personalized-learning/2017/11.

Hozien, W. 2013. "Social Media and Arab Spring Youth Identity." In *African Youth in Contemporary Literature and Popular Culture*, edited by V. Yenika-Agbaw and L. Mhando. London: Routledge.

———. 2017. *Improving Instructional Practice: Resolving Issues in Leadership through Case Studies*. Lanham, MD: Rowman and Littlefield.

———. 2020. "Addressing Microaggressions in K-12 Schools." *Education News*. Retrieved from Education Views: https://www.educationviews.org/addressing-microaggressions-in-k-12-schools/

Kamenetz, A. 2018. "The School Shootings That Weren't." *Npr.org*. https://www.npr.org/sections/ed/2018/08/27/640323347/the-school-shootings-that-werent.

Maksoud, N. 2018. "When Virtual Becomes Better than Real: Investigating the Impact of a Networking Simulation on Learning and Motivation." *International Journal of Education And Practice* 6 (4): 253–70. https://doi.org/10.18488/journal.61.2018.64.253.270

Meltzer, E. 2018. "Colorado's Superintendents Want (a Lot) More Money for Schools and a New Way to Divvy It Up." *Chalkbeat Colorado*. https://co.chalkbeat.org/2018/2/6/21104281/colorado-s-superintendents-want-a-lot-more-money-for-schools-and-a-new-way-to-divvy-it-up.

Minahan, J. 2019. *Trauma-Informed Teaching Strategies - ASCD*. ASCD. https://www.ascd.org/el/articles/trauma-informed-teaching-strategies.

Mission Statements: Where Is Your School Going? | Education World. 2015. *Educationworld.com*. https://www.educationworld.com/a_admin/admin/admin229.shtml.

National Association of Secondary School Principals. (NASSP). 2022. *Transgender Students*. https://www.nassp.org/top-issues-in-education/position-statements/transgender-students/.

National Policy Board for Educational Administration. 2015. *Professional Standards for Educational Leaders 2015*. Reston, VA: National Policy Board for Educational Administration. https://www.npbea.org/wp-content/uploads/2017/06/Professional-Standards-for-Educational-Leaders_2015.pdf

NewsOne Staff. 2018. "Ohio School District Not Allowing White Students To Flee 'Minority' Schools." *NewsOne*. https://newsone.com/3795775/ohio-school-district-white-students/.

Reyes, R. 2017. "To Be Latinx or Not to Be Latinx? For Some Hispanics That Is the Question." *NBC News*. https://www.nbcnews.com/news/latino/be-latinx-or-not-be-latinx-some-hispanics-question-n817911.

Roberts, A. 2018. "Parents Frustrated after JP Announces Charter School Lottery Do-over." https://www.fox8live.com/story/38516529/parents-frustrated-after-jp-announces-charter-school-lottery-do-over/.

Saleem, I. 2017. "Everything You Need to Know about the NAACP's Stance on Charter Schools." *Education Post*. http://educationpost.org/everything-you-need-to-know-about-the-naacps-stance-on-charter-schools/.

*Schools*. 2022. National Center for Transgender Equality. https://transequality.org/know-your-rights/schools.

Sheldon, R. 2022. "How Many Bytes for . . .?" *SearchStorage*. https://searchstorage.techtarget.com/definition/How-many-bytes-for.

Stanton, M. 2007. "Superintendents' Ethical and Legal Decision Making." *Shareok.org*. https://shareok.org/bitstream/handle/11244/7589/School%20of%20Teaching%20and%20Curriculum%20Leadership_301.pdf?sequence=1.

Steinmetz, K. 2018. "Why 'Latinx' Is Succeeding While Other Gender-Neutral Terms Fail to Catch On." *Time*. https://time.com/5191804/latinx-definition-meaning-latino-hispanic-gender-neutral/.

Texas Education Agency - 2017–2018 Accreditation Statuses. 2020. *Tea4avcastro.tea.state.tx.us*. http://tea4avcastro.tea.state.tx.us/accountability/accreditation/2017_2018_accreditation_statuses.html.

Texas School Closed After Social Media Threat Discovered. 2018. *Dfw.cbslocal.com*. https://dfw.cbslocal.com/2018/09/24/texas-school-closed-social-media-threat/.

Tsai, J. 2016. "Judge Rules for East Bay School Districts in Teacher Evaluation Lawsuit." *East Bay Times*. http://www.eastbaytimes.com/2016/09/20/judge-rules-against-requiring-standardized-test-scores-in-teacher-evaluations/.

Tucker, K. "What Are Problems That Cause Students to Drop Out of School?" https://education.seattlepi.com/problems-cause-students-drop-out-school-1412.html.

Vespa, J., L. Medina, and D. Armstrong. 2018. "Demographic Turning Points for the United States: Population Projections for 2020 to 2060." United States Census Bureau. https://www.census.gov/content/dam/Census/library/publications/2020/demo/p25-1144.pdf.

Walsh, M. 2012. "Court Rejects Teacher's Suit over Classroom Mold." *Education Week*. https://www.edweek.org/education/court-rejects-teachers-suit-over-classroom-mold/2012/03.

# About the Author

*Wafa Hozien, Ph.D.*, has been an educator and administrator for over thirty years. Presently, she serves as university administrator in the United States. Dr. Hozien uses her research and work to spark respect for the diverse people who share space on campuses, in classrooms, schools, and communities, and to prompt action for equity and justice. Her research focuses on anti-racist multicultural education, ethnic studies, and principal/superintendent preparation. She has written five books and published extensively on effective educational leadership practices that improve instructional outcomes. She is a specialist in multicultural education, diversity, and social justice education and has written widely in these fields. Research by Dr. Hozien on how educational institutions can improve race and ethnic relations has greatly influenced schools, colleges, and universities throughout the United States and the world, where she presents regularly. Most recently, she was the recipient of the Multicultural Educator of the Year Award (2017) from the State of Michigan.

www.ingramcontent.com/pod-product-compliance
Lightning Source LLC
Chambersburg PA
CBHW030122240426

43673CB00041B/1367